Shadows of the Storm

VOLUME ONE OF

The Image of War
1861-1865

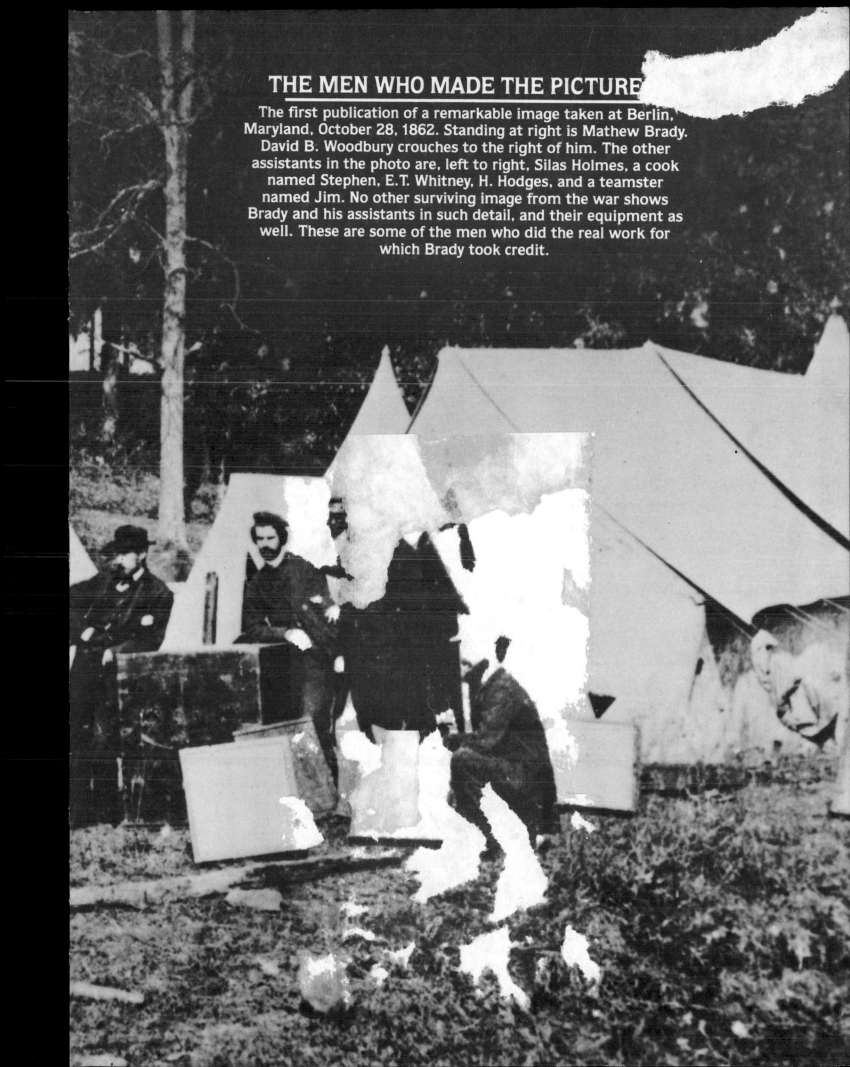

THE MEN WHO MADE THE PICTURE

The first publication of a remarkable image taken at Berlin, Maryland, October 28, 1862. Standing at right is Mathew Brady. David B. Woodbury crouches to the right of him. The other assistants in the photo are, left to right, Silas Holmes, a cook named Stephen, E.T. Whitney, H. Hodges, and a teamster named Jim. No other surviving image from the war shows Brady and his assistants in such detail, and their equipment as well. These are some of the men who did the real work for which Brady took credit.

EDITOR
WILLIAM C. DAVIS

SENIOR CONSULTING EDITOR
BELL I. WILEY

PHOTOGRAPHIC CONSULTANTS
WILLIAM A. FRASSANITO
MANUEL KEAN
LLOYD OSTENDORF
FREDERIC RAY

EDITORIAL ASSISTANTS
KAREN K. KENNEDY
DENISE MUMMERT
JAMES RIETMULDER

A Project of

The National Historical Society

Gettysburg, Pennsylvania
ROBERT H. FOWLER, Founder

EDITOR
WILLIAM C. DAVIS

SENIOR CONSULTING EDITOR
BELL I. WILEY

Shadows of the Storm

VOLUME ONE OF

The Image of War
1861-1865

DOUBLEDAY & COMPANY, INC.
GARDEN CITY, NEW YORK
1981

OVERLEAF: At the end of the long road. Samuel Cooley photographs a soldier in the ruins of Fort Sumter at the war's close. The soldier and the camera have come a long way together. (WESTERN RESERVE HISTORICAL SOCIETY, CLEVELAND, OHIO)

Cop. 2

Library of Congress Cataloging in Publication Data
Main entry under title:

Shadows of the storm.

(Image of war, 1861–1865; v. 1)
Includes index.
1. United States—History—Civil War, 1861–1865—
Pictorial works.   I. Series.
E468.7.S5   973.7'022'2
ISBN: 0-385-15466-6
Library of Congress Catalog Card Number 80–1659

Contents

A NOTE ON THE SOURCES: A credit line accompanies each photograph in this volume. Each source is written out in full when first cited, but those that contributed many photographs are thereafter abbreviated. A list of abbreviations is included at the end of the book, and we would especially like to acknowledge the generosity of the sources on this list.

Introduction

WILLIAM C. DAVIS

"A SPIRIT in my feet said 'Go' and I went." Like all true salesmen, Mathew B. Brady enjoyed a gift for overstatement. Yet in those ten words he outdid even himself, capturing the spirit of his art and of his generation during an era when the two combined to leave an indelible image of America in crisis for posterity. Mathew Brady, like over three thousand others of his kind in 1861, was a photographer. And that "spirit" in his feet sent him, and them, and their nation, to war.

By the 1860s Americans were truly fascinated with photography. The art form, and its industry, came of age just as the nation itself went mad and warred upon itself. Thus it is hardly surprising that many, and not just Brady, saw the opportunity that the Civil War afforded. During the conflict there was a steady demand in the North for "war views" in a variety of forms; cartes de visite for albums and "stereo" views for stereoscopic viewers being the most popular. In an era when printers could not yet reproduce photographs on the printed page, these views were as close as Americans could come to graphic news from the front.

With the war done, interest in it did not wane. At once the torrent of publications which fed that interest began to appear, and it continued unabated to the present. Every generation has commented on its current "wave" of renewed fascination with the Civil War, and speculated on the reason for it when, in fact, the wave began during the war and simply never stopped.

But interest in the war photographs did wane almost immediately after Appomattox. Perhaps the market had been saturated by the energetic purveyors of these images. More likely, Americans preferred not to remember the conflict they saw in the brutal reality of the photograph. Very soon myth and romanticism took the place of remembered fact. And the photos themselves were forgotten, misplaced, and worse, deliberately destroyed. Hundreds, if not thousands, of the glass negatives were sold to gardeners, not for their images, but for their glass. The precious plates were used as panes in greenhouses, the sun slowly erasing any memory of the images they once held. Others met worse fates. One man, an enterprising Mr. Bender, later claimed that he bought over 100,000 glass Civil War negatives, scraped the images from them and rendered them for their silver, then sold the glass to manufacturers of gauges and meters. Reputedly, many of them, having borne the images of one war, later carried the scenes of another, as eyepieces in gas masks worn by the doughboys in France in 1918.

For all that were lost, however, many survived, husbanded by the photographers themselves, gathered by veterans societies, hoarded by the great collectors. They were the keepers of the image, men with an appreciation—and a vision—that others lacked. Finally, just before the turn of the century, their hour, and that of their photographs, came at last. It arrived on the wings of technology, the development of the halftone printing process. At last, photographs could be easily and speedily "printed" in massive quantities. At the same time, there was a new generation of Americans who had not lived through the war, who did not feel the old pains revived by seeing the graphic destruction depicted in the photographs. The people and the image were ready for one another.

Attempts at photographic "histories" of the war began as soon as it ended, and were the work of the photographers themselves. Alexander Gardner was the first, with his 1866 publication of *Gardner's Photographic Sketch Book of the War*. Words about the war and its scenes, he said, "may not have the merit of accuracy; but photographic presentments of them will be accepted by posterity with an undoubting faith." Posterity would accept them, but not Gardner's own generation. The *Sketch Book*, each image an actual contact print made from Gardner's negatives and then pasted to the page, was financially unsuccessful. At about the same time George N. Barnard issued his 1866 *Photographic Views of Sherman's Campaign*. Priced at one hundred dollars—again to cover the expense of making sixty-one separate contact prints for each volume—Barnard's project, too, proved a commercial failure. "Those who can afford to pay one hundred dollars for a work of fine art can not spend their money with more satisfactory results than would be realized in the possession of these views," said a review, but still few copies sold.

Now, however, the laborious contact print process was no longer necessary. Halftone printing could easily produce the photographs—rather crudely, to be sure—and before long the first were published. Still, it was 1894 before a real attempt at a "photographic history" of the war appeared, George F. Williams's *The Memorial War Book*. The reproduction was somewhat primitive, and the coverage far from comprehensive. But it was a start, and several years later would appear the milestone publishing event still regarded as a classic, and by which all subsequent efforts would be measured.

In 1911 New York's Review of Reviews Company issued its mammoth ten-volume *Photographic History of the Civil War*. Its editor, Francis T. Miller, and his associates spent years in the arduous task of bringing together the thousands of images that went into their epic production. A massive correspondence with former generals and soldiers, with collectors, with historical societies, and even with some of the surviving photographers themselves, led to magnificent results. Not content with this, Miller went further and hired a recent Yale graduate, Roy M. Mason, and sent him with an almost unlimited budget through the South to search for more. "The personal touch became necessary," said Mason, "the presence of a man on the spot who could tell at a glance whether the photograph was one that was wanted, one that the history lacked." He visited more than forty southern cities. "My quarry was any and all photographs of war scenes taken by Southerners within the Confederate lines during the war." Met at least once by a shotgun and often by cold looks, still Mason encountered "the spirit of justice and tolerance" for the most part. He found treasures. In Lexington, Virginia, he found the shop of Miley, who photographed Lee on his horse Traveler. The glass plate hung in his shop window, and once each month the moon reached a position from which it shone in a skylight and through the plate and projected a gigantic figure of the mounted general on the side of a church across the street.

He found the photographs of George Cook of Charleston, who captured the image of an exploding shell in Fort Sumter and the Federal fleet as they bombarded the fortress in 1863. In the armory of Charleston's Washington Light Infantry he found images which, "when the dust of years was wiped away, . . . came out startlingly strong and clear." In Baton Rouge he met with the son of Andrew D. Lytle, who still had his father's priceless collection of views of his city under Federal occupation. In New Orleans the Washington Artillery opened up to him its own collection of portraits of men in camp and field. And so it went.

Thanks to the efforts of Mason and others like him, Miller's final production was a milestone. With thousands of photographs all reproduced from original prints, and excellent text written, often, by men who fought in the war, it instantly became the standard that no work since has managed to excel.

Nevertheless, while the passing of seven decades has not diminished the achievement of Miller and his associates, it has seriously dated their published work. By the standards of the 1980s, the reproduction in the *Photographic History of the Civil War* is primitive. Further, however able they were at flushing out the obscure image, Miller's editors were not historians. They were also prone to accept fanciful identifications given them by people who furnished prints. The result is that scores, if not hundreds, of the images they reproduced are printed over erroneous captions, errors that have been accepted and passed on by the hundreds of books since 1911 that have drawn upon Miller. Finally, and inevitably, Miller and Mason could not possibly find everything. Just as surely as they finished their tenth and last volume, new photographs were revealed that they had overlooked.

Hence, *The Image of War*. It is not conceived as a photographic history of the war. That is, frankly, impossible. Too much of the war took place in areas that had no photographers present. Whole theaters of the conflict failed to produce a single image that has survived. And in those areas that were well covered by the camera, there is still a heavy bias toward those scenes that interested the photographer or were available to him, rather than a balanced coverage of the whole.

As a result, *The Image of War* is, rather, an expression of the Civil War through the photographers' eyes. What interested them interests us. What they did not cover with their negatives, *The Image of War* does not cover in its text. The chapter narratives, written by the foremost Civil War historians of our time, aim not at a history of the war, but prepare the reader for the images to follow, and illuminate them.

And it aims to set aright a century-old injustice. Thanks to his entrepreneurial genius, Mathew Brady so left his stamp upon Civil War photography that even today the conception is widespread that Brady was the only artist covering the war, that any Civil War photograph is a "Brady." In actual fact, Brady may not personally have exposed a single one of the thousands of negatives attributed to him. By 1861 his nearsightedness had

progressed to such a state that he left all of the camera work to his assistants, while he personally took the credit. In *The Image of War* an attempt is made to return that credit to the largely forgotten men like David B. Woodbury, T. C. Roche, James Gibson, and many more, who worked for Brady. Where the actual photographer of an image published by Brady is unknown, it is identified by the firm name he used late in the war, Brady & Company, for fear that simply calling it a "Brady" may perpetuate the mistaken idea that he actually made the image himself.

Beyond correcting the record with Brady and his assistants, it is desired as well to open the readers' eyes and minds to the work—and often genius—of the host of other artists operating throughout the war-torn nation. Pioneering Confederate photographers like J. D. Edwards, F. K. Houston, J. W. Petty, and Osborn & Durbec actually predated Brady and the others, leading the way for Civil War photographers to follow. Unsung Federal artists like Samuel A. Cooley, G. H. Houghton, H. P. Moore, Haas & Peale, McPherson & Oliver, and more are given their due alongside their better-known contemporaries, Alexander Gardner and Timothy O'Sullivan. Several of these cameramen are featured in special portfolios of their work.

The research that has gone into producing the six volumes anticipated for *The Image of War* must rival that of Miller and his associates. The work of finding and collecting the images has consumed six years. Backed by the resources of the National Historical Society of Gettysburg, Pennsylvania, researchers for the project have logged more than 30,000 miles of travel, crossed the Atlantic, found images in England and Australia and at every point in between. It is conservatively estimated that slightly over 100,000 Civil War photographs have been located and personally examined. Over three hundred different sources have contributed to the series, and one hundred are represented in this first volume alone. They range from the massive 40,000-image collection of the Massachusetts Commandery of the Military Order of the Loyal Legion of the United States, now housed at the United States Army Military History Institute at Carlisle Barracks, Pennsylvania, to the smaller yet still vast collections of the Library of Congress and National Archives; to the largely untapped major collections at the Chicago Historical

Society and Cleveland's Western Reserve Historical Society; and on to the single album of war views at London's Imperial War Museum, the small, priceless holdings of several score collectors, or a single forgotten image in a small public library in Galveston, Texas. In many cases we have unconsciously followed Roy Mason's footsteps of seventy years ago. We, too, went to the armory of the Washington Light Infantry in Charleston. There we found the same photographs he did, now much more faded by time. We went to places such as Tulane University in New Orleans where, lying virtually unrecognized, rests the largest single collection of outdoor Confederate images in existence.

In its six volumes, *The Image of War* will present about four thousand photographs, over half of them published for the first time. Discovering new images was a major priority in the research for this project, a priority that has been richly rewarded. In the area of Confederate outdoor or nonstudio images, exclusive of portraits, barely one hundred were known or published prior to this undertaking. *The Image of War* will present most of those, plus over one hundred more newly discovered.

Further, extensive efforts have been made to correct the many errors and misconceptions perpetrated over the years in identifying images and their photographers. Hundreds of views appear in these volumes properly identified for the first time. And the editors made equal efforts to avoid creating new misnomers of our own.

With only one or two exceptions, all of the images here are made from original prints and, in many cases, from the actual original negatives. Research has further allowed us to select the best from several prints found of some photographs. Thus, though many of the views have been published before from damaged or faded prints, those appearing here offer them with much more clarity. In no case do we present a picture which is itself copied from a book or old halftone. This is, in a way, unfortunate, for prints of many of the photographs—particularly Confederate images by J. D. Edwards—which appeared in Miller's 1911 compilation, no longer survive. What Miller and his editors did with them is uncertain, but they are available today only in his books. The poor quality of reproduction in those volumes looks worse yet when reproduced anew, and thus we have reluc-

tantly concluded not to purloin from Miller's pages.

In a very few instances, postwar views taken a few weeks to a few years after the conflict ended have been used, but only where necessary. They are clearly identified as such. Also in the matter of identifications, we have in a few instances made careful assumptions about the artist responsible for some images based upon who was known to be working in a certain time and place.

The man-hours that have gone into this project are immeasurable, the cooperation and assistance received from our consultants and outside experts beyond calculation. Suffice it to say that, unlike Mathew Brady, we desire the credit for the contributions made to this series by hundreds of people and institutions to go where it is due.

While each photograph from the hundreds of sources consulted is individually credited, still some extra acknowledgment is due to a number of institutions and individuals who have contributed significantly to the project. Above all others we must pay tribute to the United States Army Military History Institute at Carlisle Barracks, Pennsylvania. Custodians of the mammoth collection of the Massachusetts Commandery of the Military Order of the Loyal Legion of the United States, they have made every effort to facilitate our use of this unparalleled resource. Colonel James Agnew, former director of the Institute, extended every possible courtesy and encouragement during our years of work in the collection, an attitude that prevails throughout this admirable facility.

The Chicago Historical Society holds qualitatively one of the very finest collections in the country. The Kean Archives of Philadelphia, the Kentucky Historical Society of Frankfort, and the Minnesota Historical Society of St. Paul, were equally generous. Smaller yet important collections at the New-York Historical Society in New York City and Philadelphia's War Library and Museum of the Pennsylvania Military Order of the Loyal Legion of the United States were very useful, as was the substantial photographic archive at the Western Reserve Historical Society in Cleveland, Ohio.

Important Confederate resources came chiefly from the Confederate Museum in New Orleans, the Louisiana State University Archives Department, Baton Rouge, the Pensacola Historical Society at Pensacola, Florida, and the Southern Historical Collection of the University of North Carolina at Chapel Hill. The major collections of the Museum of the Confederacy and the Valentine Museum in Richmond were indispensable. And Tulane University in New Orleans generously allowed us to mine what proved to be the richest trove of all.

In addition, scores of private collectors have done their part. Of their number, Herb Peck and his Confederate portraits were especially valuable as was Lloyd Ostendorf's widely noted holding of Lincoln and Civil War materials. Other collectors such as Ronn Palm and Wendell Lang and Robert McDonald have contributed numbers of images. To them, and to those we cannot enumerate here, we are deeply grateful.

Special mention is in order to those whose part in this undertaking has proved indispensable. To the late Bell I. Wiley, perhaps the foremost living Civil War historian, whose knowledge, advice, and indefatigable efforts as Senior Consulting Editor brought into the project the talents of the host of historians who have contributed our chapter narratives. To William A. Frassanito, our chief photographic consultant, whose immense knowledge and attention to detail in Civil War photography have created a new measure for excellence in his own books, and added mightily to the quality of this series. To Robert H. Fowler, chairman of the board of Historical Times, Inc., and founder of the National Historical Society, who shared the vision that became The Image of War and who, in six years of enormous expenditures of time and money, never once wavered or pressed that the project be finished before its time. To the editors and publishers of Doubleday & Company. Unswayed by the magnitude and expense of the undertaking, they shared as well the vision and here commence the mammoth task of capturing it for posterity.

The Image of War is not definitive. It is not intended to be. It cannot be. Rather, it is the continuation of the work commenced by the photographers themselves a century and more ago, and taken up by Francis T. Miller in 1911. Each builds upon the former. Each in turn will be built upon by those to come after. For all the errors corrected, new ones are surely made. For all the images found, more will be forthcoming. Indeed, as this first volume is delivered to the publisher "complete," another packet of time-forgotten photographs from a hitherto unknown Pennsylvania war photographer appears upon the editor's desk. And so it is incomplete. The work goes on. In generations to come, others will surely renew the quest. The reasons are plain. When an old Confederate, gazing upon a soldiers' cemetery, told Roy Mason how he loved "to watch the folks caring for their dead," Mason replied, "The whole nation cares." We are not, after all, so different from Mathew Brady. We, too, answer inner voices. A spirit in our hearts says "Seek," and we do.

The Coming of the War

T. HARRY WILLIAMS

America goes mad, and to war with itself

THE MOST SENSATIONAL NEWS in the big city newspapers of the United States in 1855 and 1856 concerned events in far-off Kansas Territory. There, according to reports of correspondents, settlers were committing widespread acts of violence on other settlers, burning and destroying property and engaging in wholesale murder. A certain amount of violence occurred in every frontier area undergoing settlement, and although this was duly recorded in the press, it did not attract special attention. What set the disorders in Kansas apart was that they resulted from, or seemed to result from, a difference in ideology between contesting individuals and groups. Kansans were not killing each other in a spirit of passion or lawlessness but in a mood of crusading zeal. They were fighting to make Kansas a free state—or a slave state. As the turmoil mounted and the deaths increased, the term "Bleeding Kansas" became a national byword.

The question of whether slavery should be permitted to enter the territories was an old one in American politics. It had first arisen in 1819 when Missouri applied for admission as a state with a constitution establishing slavery, and northern opponents of slavery and southern influence in the federal government had attempted to block admis-

sion. Although Missouri won entrance in the following year, the bulk of the then existing national domain was declared closed to slavery in the Missouri Compromise. The issue slumbered for years thereafter, but criticism of slavery continued; indeed, beginning in the 1830s more and more persons in the North began to say that slavery must be eradicated, be either abolished immediately or phased out gradually. The territorial issue reappeared in 1848 at the close of the Mexican War. As a result of that conflict, the United States had acquired a huge region to the southwest of the existing boundary, and hardly was the ink dry on the peace treaty when men in the North and the South began to argue about the status of slavery in the new possession.

As the dispute deepened, three proposals to solve the situation were advanced. Most Southerners contended that slaveholders had a constitutional right to take their human property into the recently acquired territory, or for that matter, into any part of the national domain, and to be protected in holding their property by the federal government. The most confirmed antislavery Northerners held that Congress had a constitutional power and a moral duty to exclude the institution from the new territory, or from any other territory;

"Let Freedom Ring." Symbols of American independence—Congress Hall, the Pennsylvania State House, and Philadelphia's old City Hall, in 1855. Here began the epic of American nationhood. Here, too, the Founding Fathers planted unknowingly the seeds of dissolution. (FREE LIBRARY OF PHILADELPHIA)

*It is a thriving, bustling nation, full of itself and its ever-stretching power and
prosperity. Already in 1860, Broadway in New York City is one of the busiest
streets in the world.* (U. S. ARMY MILITARY HISTORY INSTITUTE, CARLISLE
BARRACKS, PA.)

they believed that if slavery was prevented from expanding, it would ultimately die a forced death. In between these diametrically opposed views was a third formula that drew its strongest support from Democrats in the northwestern states. Known as popular sovereignty, it recommended that Congress should make no pronouncement on the status of slavery in the Mexican cession territory nor, by implication, in any other territory. Slaveholders should be permitted to enter, and the position of the institution would be determined by the territorial legislature, or, as advocates of the doctrine liked to say, by the people themselves. Although popular sovereignty did not formally exclude slavery, it was actually a subtle exclusion prescription—the majority of settlers in a territory would undoubtedly come from the more populous North.

Popular sovereignty found enough support to be enacted into law as a part of the Compromise of 1850, which attempted to settle the territorial dispute and other issues which had arisen between the sections. Comparative calm prevailed for several years after passage of the compromise act. But in 1854 Senator Stephen A. Douglas of Illinois offered a measure that stirred fresh and even more bitter controversy. The leader of the northwestern Democrats, Douglas was a believer in popular sovereignty and in the future of the West. Both principles influenced the provisions that he put into his bill. To speed settlement of the western region, he proposed to organize two new territories, Kansas and Nebraska, which lay north of the line proscribing slavery in the Missouri Compromise. But to get southern support for the bill, he had to insert a section that repealed the exclusion clause of the old and revered Missouri law, leaving the determination of the condition of slavery in the proposed territories to their legislatures. The whole North seemed to blaze with fury at passage of the Kansas-Nebraska Act. Antislavery leaders cried that the South had used its malign influence to extend its immoral institution and that this latest threat to freedom must be checked—Kansas, the southernmost of the two territories, must be settled by people from the North who would vote to make it a free state. Southern leaders responded to the challenge by urging their people to immigrate to the territory to vote for slavery. Kansas was about to become a prize to be contended for by the sections.

Many of the settlers who went to Kansas did so for the reasons that usually impelled families to move to a new area—they were looking only for a better life. But others entered to support a cause— dedicated enemies of slavery from the northeastern states and dedicated adherents of the institution from the neighboring state of Missouri who were willing to become transitory and illegal voters. Some men on both sides were not content to rely on voting to decide the issue, and soon the intimidation and the shooting started. Violence was superseding the normal democratic process.

The Kansas question stirred men to passion everywhere, including on the floors of Congress. In May 1856 antislavery senator Charles Sumner of Massachusetts delivered a bitter speech attacking various southern colleagues for supporting what he called "The Crime Against Kansas." Representative Preston Brooks of South Carolina, a younger kinsman of one of the senators attacked, was so enraged at the speech that he armed himself with a cane and went over to the other chamber and beat Sumner into bloody unconsciousness. The episode was but one of many examples of actual or threatened violence in Congress. Some members came to sessions bearing thinly concealed pistols, several fist-swinging brawls occurred between individual Northerners and Southerners or between groups, and challenges to duels were freely passed. The violence in halls dedicated to debate, like the violence in Kansas, was a symbol dark with portent for the future. Americans were becoming so aroused about the question of slavery in any of its manifestations that they were not satisfied to discuss it or to vote on it. They could relieve their feelings only by committing physical harm on those who disagreed with them. Their anger flowed in part from the contradictions in American society, a society that was homogeneous but also diverse, that was experiencing an expansion of wealth and power but was being torn apart by ideological division.

The United States in 1860 was a land of imposing physical dimensions. The writ of American authority ran from the Atlantic Ocean to the Pacific Ocean, from the Canadian border to the Mexican border. A large part of the expanse west of the Mississippi River was as yet unpeopled except by Indian tribes. A tier of states just beyond the river marked the farthest line of settlement, and beyond them was wilderness stretching to California and

Oregon on the Pacific coast. But already emigrants were pushing into the distant areas—the movement to Kansas was one example—and a constant increase in the population of the older regions gave promise that the eruptions would continue and that more states would soon be added to what popular orators liked to call "the galaxy of the Union."

The population of the thirty-three states then in the Union was approximately 31,000,000 persons, almost double the number of inhabitants in 1840. Nearly half of these lived west of the Appalachian mountain chain, a distribution that revealed the newer states were growing in influence at the expense of the older ones. Another demographic development, and at the moment a more ominous one, was the disparity in population between the free states and the slave states. The former numbered about 22,000,000 persons and the latter 9,000,000 persons of whom one third were black slaves. The South was becoming a minority, losing strength in the House of Representatives and the Electoral College every decade.

Most Americans lived, as their fathers and grandfathers had lived, in rural surroundings, on farms or in small towns. But beginning in the 1840s a significant shift of population toward cities occurred. New York City, the largest urban center, counted over 800,000 persons in 1860; Philadelphia, 565,000 persons; and Boston, 165,000. The most sensational growth was experienced by Chicago, which in little more than twenty years grew from 250 to over 100,000 inhabitants. Not participating in the trend toward urbanism was the South. If Baltimore, with its 200,000 people, is excepted as a border town, the region could boast of but one large city, New Orleans, whose 165,000 population was small in comparison with the teeming northern centers. Richmond and Charleston, next greatest in numbers, had only 40,000 each.

An increasing population was but one manifestation of national growth. Also expanding was the economy, the most dramatic and significant inflation occurring in industry. Textile, iron, and other plants dotted the Northeast, and manufacturies were beginning to spread into the Northwest and, although to a lesser extent, into the South. Accompanying the revolution in production was a revolution in transportation and communication. Railroads, superseding other means of conveyance,

laced the eastern half of the country, the greatest concentration of lines being in the Northeast and the Northwest. The effect of the coming of the railroads on American life was like that of the great technological innovations of the twentieth century —a conquest of time and space had occurred. In the 1830s a traveler required three weeks to go from New York to Chicago or St. Louis; by 1860 he could complete the trip in two to three days. The transportation revolution bound the various parts of the country into a greater if uncomfortable unity.

The section least affected by the transforming changes of the time was the South. The region below the Potomac and the Ohio stood apart, or wanted to stand apart, from the mainstream of progress. The South was still distinctive—rural, agricultural, conservative, maintaining an ordered and orderly social structure, and boasting in its plantation lords the closest approach to an American aristocracy. Above all other differences, the South was the only part of the country that contained in large numbers a race of another color than white, a race held in slavery. Southerners of all classes stood determined to uphold slavery and the system of race relations based on it against all outside attacks. Their peculiar culture, they proclaimed, was superior to that of the North. One spokesman, denouncing free society as a "monstrous abortion," described his own society as a "healthy, beautiful and natural being." The refusal of Southerners to consider any modification of their system was a key to the conflicts that rent the nation during the last half of the 1850s.

The presidential election of 1856 took place against this backdrop of continuing violence in Kansas and continuing debate over the status of slavery in the territories. The Democrats nominated James Buchanan of Pennsylvania as their candidate and offered popular sovereignty as a formula to settle the territorial question. Their opposition was a new party, the Republicans, just two years of age. The Republican organization had been formed in the anger that swept the North after the enactment of the Kansas-Nebraska Act and had absorbed most northern members of the former Whig party and some antislavery northern Democrats. The Republicans nominated as their candidate John C. Frémont of California, famous as an explorer of the Far West, and submitted as

On Saturday, October 13, 1860, J. W. Black of the firm of Black & Batchelder loaded his camera into a balloon operated by Professor Samuel A. King, and up they went, several hundred feet above Boston. There below them they captured the image of one of the principal trading cities of the world. Washington Street runs diagonally from lower right, Old South Meeting House at its other end. (U. S. AIR FORCE)

It is a nation moving west, leaving in train thousands of rural still lifes such as this unidentified scene. (JOE M. BAUMAN)

their platform congressional exclusion of slavery from all national territories. A one-idea party, they were also a sectional party, having their main strength in the North with only a smattering of support in the border slave states.

The Democrats, although troubled by sectional division, were still a national party, and they elected Buchanan and a majority to Congress. However, the young Republican party had made a surprising showing. Frémont carried eleven of the sixteen northern states and rolled up a large popular vote. A slight shift of votes in a few states would have made the sectional party the majority party.

James Buchanan was a dignified "elder statesman," almost sixty-six years of age at the time of his inauguration, and an amiable and well-meaning public servant. But he lacked resolution of character and flinched from taking strong action in a crisis. Enjoying the company of Southerners, he was inclined to let himself be guided by southern leaders. Cast into office in a period of storm, he could not have controlled all events; he rarely tried to control any of them.

Most of the crises of his administration were concerned with the issues in controversy between the sections and every outcome exacerbated sectional bitterness and moved the nation closer to dissolution. In Kansas the turmoil between the contesting factions continued unabated, with efforts now concentrated on electing a convention to write a state constitution. Buchanan used his influence to aid the proslavery side, which was clearly a minority. His action enraged Republicans and disgusted popular sovereignty members of his own party, and Congress refused to accept the con-

stitution presented by the slavery adherents. Kansas remained a territory, and an issue of discord.

At the height of the Kansas dispute the Supreme Court handed down a pronouncement on the ques-

To St. Joseph, Missouri, where immigrant trains jumped off into the Great Plains for the trek to Oregon and California. Albert Bierstadt took this 1859 view of the "Pike's Peak Passenger & Freight Express Co." (KANSAS STATE HISTORICAL SOCIETY, TOPEKA)

tion of whether slavery could enter a territory in *Dred Scott* v. *Sanford*. The case had a complicated background, but in the broadest meaning it involved the exclusion clause in the Missouri Compromise. The majority opinion (seven of the nine justices were Democrats) held that this clause was in violation of the constitutional provision that forbade Congress to take property without "due process of law." The Congress of 1820 had acted illegally in barring slavery, and no Congress could exclude the institution. Translated into the language of current politics, the decision declared the platform of the Republican party to be unconstitutional. By implication it also disallowed popular sovereignty, for if Congress could not prohibit slavery in the territories neither could a territorial legislature that was created by Congress. The voice of the highest tribunal did not calm but rather excited sectional passions. A typical Republican effusion denounced the Court as the "last resort behind which despotism is sheltered," and Republican leaders proclaimed that when their party gained control of the government they would reconstitute the Court and retry the case.

Northern anger at the Dred Scott decision was more than matched by southern rage at an event occurring in 1859. John Brown, a fierce foe of slavery who had migrated to Kansas and participated in the killings there, reappeared in the East full of a plan to strike at slavery in the South itself. With encouragement and monetary support from certain abolitionists, who realized his general purpose, he proposed to seize the Federal arsenal at Harpers Ferry in western Virginia, and from this base to incite an armed slave insurrection. In October he and eighteen followers descended on the town and captured the arsenal. No slaves came in to join him, and he was pinned down in his position by attacking citizens and local militia. News of the raid alarmed official Washington, and President Buchanan, reacting with unusual vigor, dispatched a contingent of marines under Colonel Robert E. Lee of the Regular Army to Harpers Ferry to deal with the crisis. Brown resisted the onslaught of Lee's force, but with ten of his men killed he finally had to surrender. The national government handed him over to Virginia to be tried for treason against the state.

Brown's raid aroused fury in the South, and also horror. The whites lived in constant fear of a slave uprising, and now it seemed that outside agitators, abolitionists or Republicans, had attempted to incite an insurrection. Southern suspicions were heightened by the praise heaped upon Brown by abolitionist leaders who hailed him as a saint, an "angel of light" in the words of New England writer Henry David Thoreau. Thoreau and others hoped that Brown would not escape hanging and would become a martyr to the cause of freedom. They need not have feared. Brown was duly tried and executed. In his last message to the world he wrote that he was certain the crimes of "this, guilty land" would never be purged away "but with Blood." The stage was set for the fateful presidential election of 1860.

All the boiling tensions in the country came to a head in 1860. The election in that year marked the apogee of sectionalism. Parties represented largely sectional interests, and the result prompted the South to withdraw from the Union. It is the only contest in American history in which the losing side felt that it could not live with the consequence of defeat.

The Democrats were the first to meet in convention. Gathering in historic Charleston in April, they plunged into angry debate on the issue of slavery in the territories. Southern delegates demanded that the platform affirm the right of slaveholders to take their chattels into any part of the national domain, and northern delegates held out for a popular sovereignty plank. When the latter triumphed, a number of southern delegations walked out of the hall. The managers thereupon adjourned the convention to meet again in Baltimore in June, hoping that time would cool the passions of the opposing factions. However, at Baltimore anger was even more intense, and another southern exodus occurred. The remaining delegates nominated Stephen A. Douglas to run on a popular sovereignty platform. The bolters nominated John C. Breckinridge of Kentucky to stand for the rights of slavery in the territories. There were now two Democratic parties in the field, and although each had adherents in the other section, one was a northern party and one was a southern party. The only national political organization in the country had at last split on the rock of sectionalism.

The Republicans met in bustling Chicago in May in a huge building, the Wigwam, built by the Republicans of the city to house the convention.

To Illinois expansion spread, to Galena, and a leather store run by Grant &
Perkins. Ulysses S. Grant. (CHICAGO HISTORICAL SOCIETY)

Elated at the promise of victory held out by Democratic division, the party managers were determined to present a platform and a candidate that would appeal to the broadest spectrum of northern opinion. They were especially concerned that the party should not appear to be a collection of wild-eyed crusaders who had no other objective but to attack slavery. Now the Republicans were to stand before the voters as men of moderation whose vision embraced many issues. The platform embodied the new strategy. Although reaffirming their opposition to slavery's expansion into the territories, the Republicans declared that they had no intention of interfering with the institution in the

*Northwest to Oregon went America, to Table Rock City, on stirring stories of
the Oregon Trail.* (SOUTHERN OREGON HISTORICAL SOCIETY)

*And with "California or Bust," they completed the conquest of a continent,
drawn by land, adventure, and gold. This early daguerreotype by Shaw &
Johnson shows a gold claim in the early 1850s.* (CALIFORNIA HISTORICAL
SOCIETY LIBRARY)

It was a nation thriving on commerce, whose fast clipper ships traded with the world and turned the docks at the end of New York's Wall Street into a forest of masts. (NEW-YORK HISTORICAL SOCIETY)

Trade between the states flourished, borne on iron rails and man-made waterways like the Chesapeake & Ohio Canal. (NATIONAL ARCHIVES, WASHINGTON, D.C.)

The barons of industrial expansion discovered the riches beneath the earth, and profits came to be measured in barrels. Oil Creek Valley, near Rouseville, Pennsylvania—already the scars of industry blotted the landscape. (DRAKE WELL MUSEUM, TITUSVILLE, PA.)

And the factory came to America, the sweatshop, the women and child labor, the endless days at machines producing textiles. There was great prosperity, but it cost great toil. (USAMHI)

Yet there were two Americas. While the northern states and their people pushed and built and traded and manufactured, another America took a slower pace. The South, too, had its major trading cities like Charleston, South Carolina, and to be sure, its skyline evidences a few factory smokestacks. (NYHS)

But Southerners preferred to think of themselves in a different way, as the last outpost of a more graceful, pastoral mode of life that existed more in myth than in actual memory. They thought of the beauty of Wade Hampton's garden at his plantation in Columbia, South Carolina. (USAMHI)

. . . of their river cities like Vicksburg on the mighty Mississippi. H. J. Herrick took this view from the Louisiana side of the river, Vicksburg's courthouse towering over all. (OLD COURT HOUSE MUSEUM, VICKSBURG, MISS.)

Their pride lay not in capitalism, but in cotton, piled in bales on Charleston's wharves awaiting shipment to northern and European textile mills. (WRHS)

They grudgingly gave credit to Yankee Eli Whitney's invention of the cotton gin for making possible the large-scale production and harvest of the fiber. Gin houses like this one on Edisto Island in South Carolina hummed with activity throughout the 1850s. (WRHS)

Whitney made only part of the work easy. The rest, the picking, must be done by hand, by slaves, the captive labor force of the South, the legacy of a problem the Founding Fathers chose not to solve. Timothy O'Sullivan photographed this slave family on a South Carolina cotton plantation in 1862. (LIBRARY OF CONGRESS, WASHINGTON, D.C.)

Slaves became not only a work force, but a measure of wealth as well. These belonged to Mississippi Senator Jefferson Davis. (OCHM)

They planted the fields on Pope's Plantation at Hilton Head, South Carolina. (USAMHI)

Slaves were bought and sold, and between transactions were often kept in pens like this one at Alexandria, Virginia, almost within sight of the Capitol in Washington City. (USAMHI)

They picked the cotton under the eye of their white overseers, as in this postwar image. (NA, WOMEN'S BUREAU)

And they brought their day's pickings in every evening to put it through Mr. Whitney's machine. George N. Barnard's postwar photograph was taken near Charleston, South Carolina. (NYHS)

Despite differences in their economies and ways of life, North and South still managed to accommodate each other peaceably enough in the first half of the century. Both rejoiced in the young nation's expanding horizons, and celebrated their common heroes on days like the July 4, 1859, celebration at New York Harbor. (USAMHI)

Over the nation loomed the haunting specter of sectionalism, of slavery, of southern pretensions for a nationhood of its own. South Carolina's John C. Calhoun, ardent champion of states' rights and secession, might lie dead in his tomb in Charleston, but what he stood for still lived. (USAMHI)

Sectional schism was seemingly averted in 1856 when the contest for the presidency first saw a young Republican party, northern for the most part and antislavery in character, defeated at the polls. Democrats in the South paraded horse-drawn "ships of state" in their streets. They elected their candidate, routed Republicanism, and, so they thought, ensured peace. (JMB)

Of all the men ever to hold presidential office, the people chose the one least suited. James Buchanan lacked almost everything necessary in a President, most of all a firm will and resolution. The collapse of the Union began almost at once. (NA)

Kansas came to be "Bloody Kansas" as it sought statehood. Antislave men flocked to the territory while proslave interests, fearing that the slave states would soon become a minority in Congress, did likewise. Each hoped to provide a majority to bring Kansas into statehood. The conflict between them led to open warfare on the plains, fought by units like this Free-State Battery at Topeka in 1856. (KANSAS STATE HISTORICAL SOCIETY, TOPEKA)

Violent men like James Lane led bands of marauders who proved little better than ruffians in the quest to wrest control of Kansas from their opposition. (USAMHI)

The conflict reached the floor of the United States Senate when Charles Sumner of Massachusetts, decrying the "Crime Against Kansas" in a violent antislave speech, was attacked and caned senseless by Preston Brooks of South Carolina. For three years Sumner's chair remained empty, itself a powerful symbol for the abolitionist forces. (USAMHI)

Many in the North refused to abide by the Fugitive Slave Law, part of the Compromise of 1850. When this slave, "Old Peter," nearly one hundred years old, escaped to the home of Slater Brown in Lancaster, Pennsylvania, the Quaker refused to return him to his former master.
(JMB)

The celebrated trial of Dred Scott focused even more attention on the growing rift between North and South over slavery. Despite able representation by the influential Montgomery Blair of Missouri, Scott lost his case, and his freedom.
(USAMHI)

In 1858 the battle continued in Illinois, where Stephen A. Douglas and
Abraham Lincoln vied for a Senate seat. Douglas won the election, but Lincoln
won nationwide prominence thanks to their celebrated series of debates.
Photograph by Calvin Jackson of Pittsfield, October 1, 1858. (USAMHI)

Then violence erupted at Harpers Ferry, Virginia, and the North and South were so polarized that there seemed no cementing them back together. John Brown of Ossawatomie, a free-state fighter from Kansas, led a band of men across this bridge on the Potomac, turned right, and . . . (USAMHI)

. . . *swarmed down this street to the United States Arsenal. Here they hoped to capture arms to lead a slave uprising in the South that would end slavery forever. Instead, the townspeople quickly organized against them, and Brown and his men found themselves cornered across the street* . . . (CHESAPEAKE & OHIO RAILROAD CO.)

. . . *in an engine house.* (CHESAPEAKE & OHIO RAILROAD CO.)

*Here the old man, who had grown a beard since
this 1856 photograph was made, fought
desperately, even while his sons were being killed
beside him.* (KANSAS STATE HISTORICAL SOCIETY,
TOPEKA)

(WILLIAM A. ALBAUGH)

*In Richmond, Virginia's governor issued the call for troops to suppress this
outrage, and many stepped forward. The 1st Virginia Militia, the "Richmond
Grays," answered the call. They did not take part in the final capture of
Brown, but they did arrive in Charles Town, Virginia, in time to form a hollow
square around a gallows where old John Brown was hanged after his trial. One
of their number present was John Wilkes Booth, an actor, who rather pitied
Brown, "a brave old man," he said. These four views, two of them not
previously published, show the Richmond Grays at the time of Brown's trial
and hanging.*

(VALENTINE MUSEUM, RICHMOND, VA.)

(VM)

(VM)

The man who led the capture of Brown, Colonel Robert E. Lee—a photo taken in 1851. (CHS)

THE COMING OF THE WAR

*Never was there greater pressure on the leaders in Washington to compromise,
to lead. Yet, just as they could not agree to finish the monument to the nation's
first President, so could they not agree on a course to save the country from
disunion.* (NA)

*Leadership from the Executive Mansion,
the "White House," was nonexistent. Here
Montgomery C. Meigs, the engineer
supervising the expansion of the Capitol
building, used his stereo camera to
provide a deceptively peaceful image.*
(LC)

Buchanan and his Cabinet proved hopelessly ineffectual. The two members seated at left, Jacob Thompson and John B. Floyd, were suspected of financial malfeasance. Both would become secessionists. Secretary of State Lewis Cass, behind them, had long since ceased to be a potent force in public affairs. Howell Cobb of Georgia, standing just right of Buchanan, would support secession as well. Only Joseph Holt, standing at far right, and Jeremiah Black, seated far right, were men of real force and strong Union sentiment. Isaac Toucey, seated to the left of Black, remained an unknown quantity. A divided administration could hardly unite a country. (LC)

The situation was worse at the opposite end of Pennsylvania Avenue. The Congress, like the building in which it met, seemed to be in pieces. Montgomery Meigs's photograph shows the old Capitol dome, which he would soon replace, and the partially completed new Senate wing. (LC)

The Capitol from Pennsylvania Avenue in 1860. There is still much work to be done—on the building and the Union. (LC)

Meigs's camera captures Secretary of State Cass standing at a table, and his own image in the mirror in the background. (LC)

Here compromise failed. The old House of Representatives chamber about 1861. (LC)

There the once powerful voice of Henry Clay had managed compromise from discord. But Clay's voice was stilled, and none stepped forward to take his place. (NYHS)

Instead the hotbloods took the floor, the "fire-eaters" like Senator William L. Yancey of Alabama. Dazzled by the idea of a southern nation, and perhaps their own political ambitions within it, they spurned compromise. (NYHS)

*Buchanan's Secretary of the Treasury Howell
Cobb gave the secessionists tacit support.* (LC)

*Virginia's governor Henry A. Wise, from his
experience with John Brown's raid in his own
state, felt more keenly than most the fear of slave
uprising and northern aggressions against
slavery.* (JACK MCGUIRE)

*Alexander H. Stephens, congressman from
Georgia, one-time friend of Lincoln, spoke for
those who interpreted the Constitution so strictly
that secession seemed justified, if not actually legal.*
(CHS)

Not all Southerners were fire-eaters, though. The old hero of the Texas Revolution, Sam Houston, spoke out against secession and for the Union, even at personal risk. (NA)

The fiery W. G. "Parson" Brownlow of Tennessee made strident exclamations for the Union, and published his newspaper called the Rebel Ventilator. (USAMHI)

In the midst of the sectional agitation, and largely stimulated by it, a martial spirit grew rapidly North and South. Cadets at the United States Military Academy at West Point, New York, found themselves divided, often in heated argument. From their practice batteries overlooking the Hudson . . . (LC)

. . . to their field exercises at Camp Walker, they argued and took their sides.
(LOUISIANA STATE UNIVERSITY, DEPARTMENT OF ARCHIVES AND MANUSCRIPTS, BATON ROUGE)

(USAMHI)

A bitter reminder to the southern cadets were the cannon captured during the war with Mexico a decade before. Southern soldiers contributed considerably to that war, and they had hoped to bring much of the conquered territory into the Union as slave states.

(LC)

Now young men, like these members of the class of 1864, pondered just what their budding military careers held for them, and who their first battles would bring against them. Standing at left is Ranald MacKenzie, soon to be a general, and in years to come a noted Indian fighter in the West. (USAMHI)

The old Regular Army was undermanned, ill equipped, and officered largely by men with no real combat experience, and those that did know battle were acquainted with a kind of war that would never be fought again. Colonel Joseph Plympton and his black orderly. (PEARL KORN)

Even less experienced were the volunteer and militia units springing up everywhere. What they lacked in field knowledge, they made up for in natty attire and precision at drill. Here officers of the 6th New York State Militia and, standing second from the left, E. Elmer Ellsworth, in July 1860. A favorite of Abraham Lincoln, Ellsworth led one of the North's finest drilled units, his "Fire Zouaves." (CHS)

Cincinnati, Ohio's "Guthrie Grays," ready for the foe, whoever it might be. (CINCINNATI HISTORICAL SOCIETY)

And in the South men like Hamilton McDevit Branch of the Oglethorpe Light Infantry paraded in their military finery. (HERB PECK, JR.)

The Mobile Cadets from Alabama refined their marksmanship. (HP)

THE COMING OF THE WAR

*And in Louisville, Kentucky, in August 1860, the State Guard held a much
publicized encampment. The holiday atmosphere of it all, with a refreshment
stand and ice cream, barely concealed the rattling sabers.* (KENTUCKY HISTORICAL
SOCIETY, KENTUCKY MILITARY HISTORY MUSEUM, FRANKFORT, KY.)

By 1860, the last remaining hope of maintaining the Union was the Democratic party. Friendly to southern interests, it could keep the South in the nation if it stayed united and defeated the Republicans in November. Instead, the party fragmented. The chiefly northern wing nominated Stephen A. Douglas, the "Little Giant" of Illinois. Immensely popular, he still came in last in the electoral ballot. (USAMHI)

The more conservative Northerners and the southern rights men nominated Buchanan's Vice-President, John C. Breckinridge of Kentucky. The only candidate with nationwide appeal, his popular vote was evenly divided between North and South, but he placed second in the Electoral College. (LC)

The Republicans, in the face of a Democratic split, were ensured of success. New York's William H. Seward, standing at left, had hoped for the nomination, but he lost it to Douglas's old foe from Illinois . . . (NYHS)

. . . Abraham Lincoln. In June 1860 photographer Alexander Hesler of Chicago captured Lincoln just after his nomination. Friends regarded it as the best portrait of Lincoln ever made. In November he became the sixteenth President of the United States. (KEAN ARCHIVES, PHILADELPHIA)

Elected with him, as Vice-President, was Hannibal Hamlin of Maine. (USAMHI)

Shortly after his nomination for the Presidency, a still beardless Lincoln unbends his lanky frame for a full-length portrait in his home town of Springfield, Illinois. (LC)

Their election brought jubilation in much of the North, as in Mohawk, New York, where the "Mohawk Wide Awakes" and their band paraded in honor of the victory. (LLOYD OSTENDORF COLLECTION)

*But there was no rejoicing in Charleston, South Carolina. Despite Lincoln's
earnest promises not to interfere with slavery where it already existed,
Southerners saw in his election a dagger poised at their labor system, their way
of life, and their honor.* (NYHS)

*Animated by years of heated rhetoric, exaggerated
fears and hatreds, irresponsible politicians, and an
impulse for southern nationalism, South Carolina
called a convention here in Secession Hall. The
outcome was never in doubt. In December 1860
they adopted here an ordinance of secession. The
broadsides on the streets the next day read "The
Union Is Dissolved."* (USAMHI)

Six other states did the same in the weeks to follow,
and on February 18, 1861, in Montgomery,
Alabama, new capital of the Confederate States
of America, they inaugurated their first President,
Jefferson Davis of Mississippi. A. C. McIntyre of
Montgomery sensed something historic taking
place, and set his camera to capture the scene. The
Alabama statehouse clock says 1 P.M. Davis and
Howell Cobb stand at the doorway between the
center columns. The Confederacy is begun. (NA)

Jefferson Davis, photographed in 1859 by
Montgomery Meigs. An unpublished portrait which
shows him with a hint of a smile. After 1860 he
would rarely smile again. (LC)

*In the North, four days after Davis's inauguration, President-elect Lincoln
arrived in Philadelphia. Here, on Washington's birthday, he symbolically raised
the flag at Independence Hall. The Union, he promised, would be preserved.
Frederick D. Richards caught the scene with his camera while the dignitaries
stood at prayer. Lincoln is visible directly above the star on the left of the flag,
while men view the scene from trees.* (LO)

*And on March 4, 1861, a crowd gathered before
the stands on the Capitol steps in Washington.
Meigs set his camera to record the scene.* (LC)

(LC)

(LC)

Then Lincoln took the oath of office and told the nation that the Union must be preserved. "We are not enemies, but friends," he told the South. "We must not be enemies." "In your hands, my dissatisfied fellow-countrymen, and not in mine, is the momentous issue of civil war." Meigs certainly could not have heard the President, but his camera caught the moment forever. (LC)

. . . to a firebrand Unionist in Missouri, Nathaniel
Lyon. (USAMHI)

. . . to a professor at the Virginia Military
Institute, seen here in Mexican War uniform,
Thomas Jonathan Jackson. (USAMHI)

. . . to a young southern officer, Ambrose Powell
Hill. (MUSEUM OF THE CONFEDERACY)

. . . to a dashing Virginian who had helped Lee
corner John Brown, James Ewell Brown Stuart.
(CONFEDERATE MUSEUM, NEW ORLEANS)

. . . to men like Captain A. W. Reynolds.
(USAMHI)

. . . to a sour, humorless, Mexican War veteran,
Braxton Bragg. (SOUTHERN HISTORICAL
COLLECTION, UNIVERSITY OF NORTH CAROLINA,
CHAPEL HILL)

And to Charleston went the word. It was in their hands, said Lincoln. (LC)

In the hands of Brigadier General Pierre G. T. Beauregard, commanding the Confederates gathered in Charleston. (OCHM)

And in their hands were guns trained on an island of masonry in the middle of Charleston Harbor, Fort Sumter. (LOUISIANA HISTORICAL ASSOCIATION, SPECIAL COLLECTIONS DIVISION, TULANE UNIVERSITY)

The Guns at Fort Sumter

W. A. SWANBERG

A Charleston April shatters America's innocence

"I HAVE THE HONOR TO REPORT," Major Robert Anderson wrote on December 26, 1860, after his night-shrouded move across a mile of water to Fort Sumter, "that I have just completed, by the blessing of God, the removal to this fort of all my garrison." The anger which this clandestine shift of a mere seventy-odd men caused in the South, and the joy it aroused in the North, bespoke the sectional strife of which the major and the Charleston forts had become a symbol.

President Buchanan saw in it none of God's work. "Are calamities never to come singly!" he lamented. Yearning to finish his nine remaining weeks in office and to leave the secession crisis in the lap of the man who had caused it, Lincoln, he had said that there would be no "hostile act" in the harbor. Three South Carolina commissioners, just arrived in Washington to parley about the forts, said Anderson's move *was* a hostile act. Mississippi Senator Jefferson Davis, soon to be Confederate President, told the President, ". . . you are surrounded with blood and dishonor on all sides." Exultant headlines in the North and outraged ones in the South told the real significance of the major's action. Secretary of War John B. Floyd telegraphed Anderson in anger:

Intelligence has reached here this morning that you have abandoned Fort Moultrie, spiked your guns, burned the carriages, and gone to Fort Sumter. . . . Explain the meaning of this report.

But Floyd was a Virginian who had been implicated first in a financial scandal and then in an effort to ship cannon from Pittsburgh to southern points, where they would be useful to the new Confederacy if it came to war. Buchanan had asked him to resign. Floyd had not yet got around to it. His continued presence in the Cabinet was one of the errors of a lame-duck President whose power to govern had virtually become paralyzed. Floyd had sent Anderson to Charleston in the first place because of the major's background as a Kentuckian who had married a Georgia girl, had until recently owned a few slaves, and expressed a sympathy for the South equaled only by his reverence for the Union. At Moultrie he had been deserted by the secretary—left in an untenable fort without reinforcements, his requests for instructions usually ignored. Moultrie, in the midst of extensive repairs, had gaps in its walls entered by neighborhood dogs, children, or secessionist leaders who watched, took notes and photographs, and called the Union presence there "coercion." From secessionist homes overlooking the fort it would be possible for snipers to pick off cannoneers. A well-armed force could overpower the garrison. Anderson's father, Major Richard Clough Anderson, had defended Moultrie against the British in 1779 and been captured— one particular footstep the son preferred not to follow in. He was aroused by Charlestonian threats and insistence that the forts be handed over, noting, "They are making every preparation (drilling nightly, &c) for the fight which they say must take place and insist on our not doing anything."

Indeed, few outsiders could gauge the Carolinian intensity. Francis J. Pickens had learned this when he returned from a recent tour as minister to Russia, talked with his good Democratic friend Buchanan in the White House, agreed that the Palmetto people were being hasty, and said he would quiet them when he got home. But Pickens, immediately running for governor of the state, found his moderating speeches so disdained that he quickly became a hotspur and was elected. Now, with Anderson in Sumter, the governor seized Moultrie, the United States arsenal (with 22,000 muskets), the customs house, and post office.

That was an error, for the chances were good that if Pickens had only protested, Buchanan would have ordered Anderson back to Moultrie. Now, if the President did such a thing, he would be hanged in effigy in a hundred northern cities and probably impeached. And now he was confronted by Secretary Floyd, whom he considered already fired, coming to him and resigning because of the President's "dishonorable" acceptance of the move to Sumter—a wily exit indeed. And when the South Carolina commissioners left after calling Buchanan lying and deceitful, he seemed more affected by this insult to his person than by the various discourtesies to the Union. Anderson, he said heavily, would have to be reinforced.

At Sumter, Chaplain Mathias Harris led a prayer of thanksgiving. Major Anderson raised Old Glory with slow dignity. The band played "Hail, Columbia" as the battery presented arms, then the men broke into spontaneous cheers, both in enthusiasm for their leader and in relief at escaping Moultrie. Yet, while it was true that Sumter was entirely surrounded by water, four times as big as Moultrie, and planned for three tiers of 146 guns served by 650 men, it was anything but impregnable in its present condition. Work on the fort had been im-

peded by the current quarrels. The barracks were unfinished, only fifteen guns had been mounted, many embrasures were wide open, the parade was choked with building materials as well as 5,600 shot and shell and sixty-six unmounted guns. The place could have been taken by a few hundred men with scaling ladders. Luckily, this was not known in town. "Twenty-five well-drilled men could hold it against all Charleston," said the Charleston *Courier* in dismay.

The garrison began mounting more guns. Abolitionist officers such as Captain Abner Doubleday and Captain John G. Foster, who had suspected Anderson of excessive southern sympathies, praised the skillful move to Sumter, and morale was high until the *Star of the West* arrived from New York on January 9 with two hundred men and supplies for the garrison. It was typical of the confusion and irresolution in government that the men were sent in a rented, unarmed merchantman rather than a Navy warship, and that Major Anderson had not been informed of its dispatch whereas the Charlestonians had. Buchanan's secessionist Secretary of the Interior, Jacob Thompson of Mississippi, had telegraphed the news to Governor Pickens and then resigned his post. Anderson was utterly perplexed when the vessel hove into view and was fired on by one of the Carolina batteries— arguably the first shot of the War Between the States, fired by a young cadet named George E. Haynsworth. Other batteries let fly, with aim mostly poor. Anderson, whose orders had been to act "strictly on the defensive," had his gunners ready but so longed for an amicable settlement between the states that he was loath to give the order to fire. As he pondered, the *Star* took two minor hits and fled. Doubleday and others were incensed at this failure to defend the flag, whereas soldiers with southern sympathies, such as Lieutenant R. K. Meade, thought Anderson's restraint wise. As for the fire-eating Robert Barnwell Rhett's Charleston *Mercury,* it hailed the striking of the first blow, saying, "It has wiped out a half century of scorn and outrage."

Governor Pickens was in the odd position of heading a self-styled South Carolina republic that still used United States stamps. Its congressmen were using their franking privileges to propagandize for the new Confederacy, and Pickens himself was asking for a $3,000 balance due him as min-

The ghostly face of Fort Sumter in Charleston Harbor, almost lost in this scratched and faded ambrotype. It is the only known photo of the fortress before its bombardment. (VM)

ister to Russia, although he had forbidden the U. S. Subtreasury in Charleston to cash any more drafts from Washington. That cost him dearly when Washington, with intentional irony, sent him a $3,000 draft on the Subtreasury whose payments he had stopped. Pickens sent out his secretaries of state and war, Judge A. G. Magrath and General D. F. Jamison, under a flag of truce to urge Anderson to look to his own safety and evacuate Sumter peacefully since, they said, the United States government itself was crumbling. The major declined, urged diplomacy with Washington, and kept his men at the task of mounting more guns. Meanwhile, Colonel Samuel Colt of Hartford was shipping thousands of firearms south and building himself a mansion, and a Connecticut munitions firm sold 300,000 pounds of powder to Governor Pickens. Treason? Not at all. Did not the President himself declare that the seceded states were still part of the Union?

"The people of the South are mad," old Lewis Cass said; "the people of the North are asleep. The President is pale with fear. . . . God only knows what is to be the fate of my country!"

With South Carolina spending $20,000 daily for defense, and shipping now avoiding its greatest harbor, bankruptcy became a threat. Yet other southern leaders urged Pickens to go slowly, arguing that northern Democrats would sustain Buchanan whereas if a confrontation could be delayed until Lincoln took office, the Democrats would oppose him and the North would be divided. A new voice in Washington was that of William Henry Seward, Secretary of State–designate for Lincoln, who let it be known that he had plans (as yet unspecified) to resolve the whole quarrel and save the Union too. Other voices rumored that secessionists plotted to seize the capital on February 13, when the electoral votes would be officially counted and Lincoln formally declared the winner. They inspired the aged, Virginia-born General Winfield Scott, head of the Army, to colorful utterance:

> I have said that any [such person] should be lashed to the muzzle of a 12-pounder and fired out of a window of the Capitol. I would manure the hills of Arlington with fragments of his body. . . . It is my duty to suppress insurrection—*my duty!*

The day passed without incident. Buchanan's severity had given way once more to caution. He had swallowed the *Star of the West* affront. He wavered about reinforcing Anderson at all. He hoped that the new Confederate government would be less demanding than Pickens, that the crisis could be put off for his remaining days in the White House. On the complaint of Southerners that it was "warlike," he was ready to cancel a Washington's Birthday parade of six hundred soldiers until the spirited New York Congressman Daniel Sickles exploded that Washington was a Virginian, a national hero. The President was, critics said, ready to "give up part or even the whole of the Constitution to save the remainder."

Lincoln arrived quietly next day, having taken an earlier train to foil a rumored plot to assassinate him. The delegates from the seceded states had already met in Montgomery, elected Jefferson Davis president, and taken pains to remove the question of the forts from the excitable Pickens, who was now only a governor again. The men at Sumter froze in a heatless fort and ran low on tobacco while the aristocratic Carolinians enjoyed madeira, champagne, Spanish cigars and spoiled for a fight. Major Pierre Beauregard, U.S.A., recently deprived of his post as commander at West Point because of his southern allegiance, arrived in Charleston to take charge as Brigadier General Beauregard, C.S.A. He had been Anderson's pupil when the latter taught gunnery at West Point. He respected his one-time teacher but soon realized that he could overpower or starve out the meager Sumter garrison if he could prevent its reinforcement. Anderson, the man of honor, was wrestling also with the problem of what he should do in case his own state of Kentucky seceded, in which event it seemed to him that no matter what course he took there would be dishonor involved. A popular ditty in the North ran:

Brigadier General Pierre G. T. Beauregard, commanding Confederate forces in and around Charleston. He appears in his uniform as colonel of engineers in the Provisional Army of Louisiana, shortly after the time he served briefly as superintendent of the Military Academy at West Point. Filled with grand ideas of warfare—and his potential part in it—this Creole officer looked forward to firing on Fort Sumter as soon as the authorities gave him the word. (USAMHI)

> James is in his Cabinet
>   Doubting and debating;
> Anderson's in Sumter,
>   Very tired of waiting.
>
> Pickens is in Charleston,
>   Blustering of blows;
> Thank goodness March the Fourth is near,
>   To nip Secession's nose.

On the fourth, Lincoln gave his inaugural in a city bristling with police and soldiers against a threatened secessionist coup, saying among other things, ". . . no state, upon its own mere notion, can lawfully get out of the Union," and "The power confided in me will be used to hold, occupy and possess the property and places belonging to the government." He had earlier said more colorfully that the Union was not a "free love arrangement" which any state could repudiate at will. The new Confederate commissioners arrived in Washington to parley with Lincoln through an intermediary, since the President would not recognize the C.S.A. Secretary Seward launched into an irresponsible and unauthorized course, letting the commissioners know that Lincoln was untutored in national affairs but that he, Seward, would soon bring him around and that Sumter would be peacefully evacuated. Seward's policy was based on his certainty that there was great innate love for the Union in the South and that if the states were permitted to secede, this love would combine with loss of trade and internal bickering to make them clamor to rejoin the Union within a year or so.

A message from Major Anderson staggered the new administration, for it told of the steady buildup of Confederate forces, the fact that Sumter had supplies for less than forty days, and gave an estimate (in which Anderson's officers substantially agreed) that it would take reinforcements of 20,000 men to hold the fort.

Twenty thousand men! No such force was available, nor were there enough Navy men-of-war to carry them if there had been. General Scott, much under Seward's influence, agreed with Anderson's estimate and told Lincoln, "Evacuation seems almost inevitable."

The idea was repugnant to the President. It would violate his "hold, occupy and possess" promise in his inaugural. It would begin his administration with a surrender which not even the irresolute Buchanan had contemplated. It would outrage the North and subject him to the contempt of the South—indeed, the whole watching world. Seward pressed him with the evacuation idea and the theory of an affectionate South which, if given its way, would spring back into the Union as if on a rubber band—a theory Lincoln deeply suspected. Determined to get the facts, he sent Gustavus Vasa Fox, a former Navy captain who yearned to lead an expedition to reinforce Anderson, to Charleston to confer with the major and find the actual condition of the fort and garrison. He dispatched Ward Lamon and Stephen Hurlbut separately to Charleston to sound officials and private citizens

His antagonist, Major Robert Anderson, commanding in Fort Sumter. A native of Kentucky, Anderson's sympathies were severely torn by the sectional crisis, but he saw his duty to the Union as paramount. (USAMHI)

and see if they were, as Seward supposed, affectionate Unionists in a temporary fit of bad temper.

There were signs of spring in Charleston, ladies and gentlemen were promenading on the Battery, and the rumor that Sumter would soon be evacuated—which had appeared in the local papers—added spice to the air. The Army in South Carolina now numbered ten regiments of 8,835 men. Local photographers did a large business perpetuating the likenesses of these young men in their new uniforms. One photographer, George Cook, went to Sumter and persuaded the officers to sit for a group portrait despite Doubleday's conviction that he was a spy. In the city there was a magnificent St. Patrick's Day parade, and the feeling toward Anderson and his tobaccoless and short-rationed men softened enough so that cigars and several cases of claret were sent out for the officers. Captain Fox was permitted to visit Anderson and to observe, without mentioning it to the major, that reinforcement of the fort appeared feasible if done skillfully in darkness. Ward Lamon, Lincoln's close friend, apparently believed that there was now no choice but to quit Sumter, for he clearly gave Governor Pickens that impression and, on visiting Anderson at the fort, left him with the conviction that he would be withdrawn. Hurlbut, a native of Charleston who was now an Illinois lawyer, devoted himself to a survey of relatives and friends he had in the city. He decided that Seward's theory was absurd, that "there is a unanimity of sentiment" against the Union that was deep and unrelenting.

It is doubtful that there was ever so important an issue on which there was so much disagreement, so many misinterpretations and errors, so many men at cross purposes, often utterly mistaken and snarled in confusion.

Anderson was relieved that the issue, as he now believed, was to be settled by his withdrawal and that war would be averted. But as the days passed in Charleston (where there were rumors that the major had resigned his commission and that Captain Doubleday had gone insane and was in irons), impatience grew at the failure of the garrison to decamp. General Beauregard, hearing talk that

Castle Pinckney in Charleston. Here and at other works like this, the Confederate volunteers gathered during the early months of 1861, to train and await the time of their taking the Yankee fort that taunted them in their own harbor. (VM)

demolition charges might be left in Sumter, wrote Anderson to suggest discreetly that the fort be left undamaged when he departed. The Confederacy in Montgomery was angry at the delay. In Sumter, the garrison was ready to pack and go north where pork chops, apple pie, and beautiful women were realities instead of dreams. Sumter was down to its last barrel of flour, as Anderson reported on April 3 to the new Secretary of War, Simon Cameron, urgently asking instructions. No instructions came.

The Confederate commissioners in Washington now found through an intermediary that Seward was no longer certain that Sumter would be evacuated. The secretary had done his best to impose his policy on the new President and, in failing, had caused misunderstanding and provoked accusations of bad faith. On April 8, a messenger from Lincoln handed Governor Pickens a paper whose single sentence exuded blunt honesty:

I am directed by the President of the United States to notify you to expect an attempt will be made to supply Fort Sumter with provisions only, and that if such attempt be not resisted, no effort to throw in men, arms or ammunition, will be made, without further notice, or in case of an attack upon the Fort.

At the same time, Anderson received his first instructions from the new administration: an expedition would attempt to supply him "and, in case the effort is resisted, will endeavor also to reinforce you." He had reconciled himself to his mortifying failure to defend the *Star of the West* on the ground that he had saved the peace. Now he had mortification and war too. As for Sumter's men, to whom their fort had become a prison, they reacted with a kind of glorious cussedness and cheered lustily at the news that they would have a chance to throw iron at the Carolinians who had made their lives so difficult.

Anderson declined a last offer by Beauregard permitting him to salute his flag if he would leave peacefully. With food left for perhaps sixty hours, he put his men on stern rations. The Carolinians now had at least thirty guns and eighteen mortars bearing on Sumter from six widely separated emplacements, some of which Sumter could not touch. To save his men, the major ordered them to serve only the guns in the more protected casemate tier, which limited them to twenty-one guns, most

Probably Confederates lounging inside Castle Pinckney, ready to fill its cannon with the shot stacked all about them and send the missiles on their way to Sumter. (SOUTH CAROLINA HISTORICAL SOCIETY)

of them only 32-pounders, and not a single mortar.

The first shot on Fort Sumter was fired from Fort Johnson on James Island at 4:30 A.M. April 12, 1861. It woke up Doubleday, who commented, "[It] seemed to bury itself in the masonry about a foot from my head." He stayed in bed as the firing became an intermittent roar. Sumter did not answer until after 6 o'clock reveille and a breakfast consisting of fat pork and water. "Be careful of your lives," Anderson cautioned, ordering his men to stay in the casemates as much as possible. Doubleday, his second in command, was given the honor of firing the first shot against the rebellion—one he accepted with zest, reflecting, "To me it was simply a contest, politically speaking, as to whether virtue or vice should rule." Private John Carmody, knowing that the bigger barbette guns above were loaded and aimed at Moultrie, disobeyed orders, stole up there, and fired them one by one, making a great noise but with little effect on the well-protected Confederate batteries. It was an unequal battle, what with Sumter's lack of mortars and inability to fire shell (there were no fuses), not to mention the poor provender. Enemy fire, gaining in accuracy,

The Charleston Zouave Cadets in Castle Pinckney, smart, well equipped, and anxious. (USAMHI)

cleared the parapet and started fires in the wooden barracks inside, which took smart work to extinguish. Sumter's most visible achievement was a ball that crashed into the large frame Moultrie House hotel, which sent dozens of battle-watchers scurrying.

Early in the afternoon a Sumter watchman saw a United States man-of-war far out beyond the bar. Reinforcements and food! A shout of joy went up from the exhausted gunners—all in vain. The expedition led by Captain Fox had been broken up by confusion in New York and by a storm that drove two of its fighting ships and its tugs off course. The tugs were the heart of Fox's careful plan for reaching the fort, and the guns were essential to protect the tugs. Fox was waiting for help that never came.

The Sumtermen loosed curses the next morning when they saw the "rescue" vessels still waiting in the distance. Cartridges got so low that they restricted their firing to one gun every ten minutes. The barracks took fire again so that there was no

putting it out. Flames crept slowly toward the magazine where 275 barrels of powder were stored. The magazine was banked with earth for protection, but flying embers touched off stockpiles of shells and grenades that had been placed at strategic spots along the gorge wall, sending down showers of sparks and broken masonry. The main gates were now ablaze. Smoke poured into the casemates, choking the men serving the guns. From the shore the smoke and flame made it seem impossible that Sumter could continue the battle, and there was Carolinian admiration when its guns kept firing. Texas Senator Louis Wigfall, now a Confederate colonel, who had damned the Union and cheered the attack, marveled at this display of courage but thought it had gone far enough. He got a boat and was rowed to the fort, unseen by the smoke-blinded defenders. He entered an open embrasure, carrying a white flag on his sword, and came upon a sooty-faced Major Anderson, whose coolness astonished him.

"You have defended your flag nobly, sir," Wigfall shouted. "It's madness to persevere. . . . General Beauregard wishes to stop this, and to ask upon what terms you will evacuate this work."

Anderson at length agreed to parley. Only three cartridges remained. His men were spent. The larder was all but empty. There was danger of explosions in the fort. The effort to reinforce him had somehow collapsed. It would indeed be madness to persevere.

After thirty-three hours of bombardment, the Sumter flag went down at 1:30 P.M. April 13. A few men on each side had been injured by flying debris, but the only fatality of battle was a horse killed on Morris Island by a Sumter ball. Charleston was in transports over the victory. Headlines in the North used the word "WAR." Young men, North and South, began flocking to the banners. It was, as Horace Greeley said later, a comparatively bloodless beginning for the bloodiest conflict America ever knew.

Lieutenant R. C. Gilchrist, standing second from the left, carries a sword more like a scimitar than a saber, but the cadets in their pipe-clayed crossbelts dare not smile. Neither do their black orderlies at the rear. A year before most southern states had statutes on their books preventing slaves from reading or gathering together. Now they were uniformed and sometimes even trusted with arms as they came to the front to see to life's amenities while their masters met the enemy. (VM)

Some military organizations that existed before the war, as much fraternal groups as real armed units, readied for the coming fight. Prominent were the men of Charleston's own Washington Light Infantry. They bivouacked in Camp Truesdale on the east end of Sullivan's Island. This faded old print shows their officers before their tent, equipped in a manner that two years hence would be only a fond memory. (WASHINGTON LIGHT INFANTRY)

Another group of Confederates in Charleston, fully equipped for the field, their knapsacks on their backs, their Harpers Ferry rifles on their shoulders. (VM)

Simon Cameron, Lincoln's Secretary of War, was slow in appreciating Anderson's helpless situation at Sumter, and slower still in doing anything about it. (USAMHI)

OCEOLA

Patriot and Warrior

Died at Fort Moultrie

January 30th, 1838

Reminder of an earlier brave, now buried at Fort Moultrie. Osceola, the
Seminole leader, effectively defeated the U. S. Army's attempt to subdue his
people until the government admitted that it had lost the contest. His example
was hardly lost on the high-spirited Southrons gathered at Charleston. (VM)

Secretary of State William Seward played several
ends against the middle in attempting to avoid the
outbreak of hostilities in Charleston. In so doing he
lied, overstepped his authority, and severely tried
the patience of Lincoln. (USAMHI)

*Hurt most by Seward's interference was septuagenarian Lieutenant General
Winfield Scott. Once the foremost soldier of the young republic, he was now an
obese old man, a picture of ruined magnificence. Yet his mind was as active as
ever, and he appreciated at once the hopelessness of reinforcing Anderson in
Sumter without precipitating war. He advised that the fort be evacuated.
Lincoln would not have it. (KA)*

*And that left Major Robert Anderson caught
squarely in a trap. Charleston photographer George
Cook took his camera out to Sumter in February
1861 and persuaded Anderson and his officers to
sit for him. A tongue-in-cheek broadside soon
appeared describing how "Col. George S. Cook, of
the Charleston Photographic Light Artillery,"
stormed Sumter, "heroically penetrated to the
presence of Maj. Anderson, and levelling a
double barrelled Camera, demanded his
unconditional surrender." The broadside appeared
under the headline, "*MAJOR ANDERSON TAKEN*!"
It looked like war was going to be fun. (VM)*

Anderson and his officers "captured" by Cook. Most of them would be heard from in the war to come. Seated from the left are Captain Abner Doubleday, Anderson, Surgeon Samuel W. Crawford, and Captain John G. Foster. Standing from the left are Captain Truman Seymour, Lieutenant G. W. Snyder, Lieutenant Jefferson C. Davis, Lieutenant R. K. Meade, and Captain T. Talbot. All but Snyder, Meade, and Talbot will become generals. (USAMHI)

Talbot, Crawford, and Seymour posed separately, enjoying the distinction of being "captured" twice. (USAMHI)

There were those who would help Anderson, and finally a relief expedition was sent, led by Gustavus V. Fox, Assistant Secretary of the Navy. But it could not dare Charleston's guns, and so it sat on the horizon, within sight but not reach of Anderson's exhausted command. (NAVAL PHOTOGRAPHIC CENTER)

*The Confederates, from their lookout tower at Fort Washington, expected
Fox's coming. Several of them are here waving their caps in celebration,
perhaps at the Union fleet's failure to test their batteries.* (WASHINGTON LIGHT
INFANTRY)

*And finally came war. At 4:30 A.M., or shortly
after, April 12, 1861, a signal gun was fired from
Fort Johnson. Seconds later Edmund Ruffin,
fire-eating secessionist from South Carolina, jerked
a lanyard . . .* (NA, BRADY COLLECTION)

. . . on one of these eight-inch columbiads in the Iron Clad Battery moored off Morris Island, and launched one of the first hostile shots of the war against Sumter's parapet.

A rare, previously unpublished photograph by Osborn & Durbec of Charleston showing the interior of the Iron Clad Battery, taken April 17, 1861, just five days after the firing. One of these guns, or a third not shown, fired Ruffin's hostile shot. (CHS)

The first answering Federal shot of the war was fired by Captain Doubleday, who gladly sent a ball toward the Iron Clad Battery, though it bounced harmlessly off its roof. (USAMHI)

The Surgeon Crawford began firing his gun, sending his shells toward an unusual and ungainly apparition . . . (USAMHI)

The iron-sheathed Floating Battery at Sullivan's Island mounted two
42-pounder cannon and two 32-pounders, and proudly flew the flag of the
new Confederacy overhead. A photograph taken on April 16, 1861, by an
unidentified photographer, shows the Floating Battery in position off the island.
This print has not been published in nearly seventy years. (VM)

After thirty-three hours of bombardment, former
Senator Louis T. Wigfall of Texas, aide to
Beauregard and an ardent secessionist, carried a
truce flag to Sumter and asked Anderson to
surrender. Seeing the hopelessness of further
resistance, the major gave up. (CIVIL WAR TIMES
ILLUSTRATED)

*On April 14, Anderson and his command left the fort to its conquerors. The flag
of the Confederate States of America went up a makeshift staff, and the next
day photographer F. K. Houston of 307 King Street in Charleston became the
first to bring a camera into Fort Sumter. Elated soldiers feigned action poses
while he made his slow exposure, but the proud new flag would not stay still.*
(USAMHI)

That day and in those following, several cameramen came to the fort. The names of some are now lost, but thankfully not their photographs. One of them, probably Osborn & Durbec, made a panorama from three separate images of Sumter that shows vividly the damage done by Beauregard's batteries. They claimed to have made these shots the very day of the surrender. (USAMHI)

Sumter's eastern terreplein and parapet, April 15, 1861. Just over the wall can be seen a steam sidewheeler that transported more and more Confederates into the captured fort, and sightseers from Charleston as well. One such is the top-hatted man standing at right. The man at left is Major Nathan G. Evans, who will shortly be a brigadier general at Bull Run. The man in the middle is Lieutenant Robert Pringle. (CHARLESTON LIBRARY SOCIETY)

But Anderson's men did some damage, too, and the camera artists were not loath to show it. Here on April 16 the soldiers' barracks at Fort Moultrie showed the effect of Sumter's fire. (CHARLESTON Post-Courier)

So, too, did Moultrie's northwest angle. (CHARLESTON MUSEUM)

*April 15, the interior of Sumter, showing the destroyed western barracks and,
in the right foreground, columbiads that Anderson had mounted in the ground
to use as mortars.* (VM)

April 15, the southwest angle of the fort, a panorama formed of two separate images. Dressed smartly on parade, the conquering Confederates line up for the camera, while their flag floats gently overhead. Anderson built the earth bank at left to protect the lower tier of soldiers' quarters. The fort's beacon lantern, removed from its place on the parapet, rests in the parade ground. These two images have never before been juxtaposed to give this wide view of the interior of the fort. (VM)

April 15, another view of the southwest angle showing officers' quarters and soldiers' barracks. Elated Confederates stand in groups retelling their experiences while watching the bombardment. (VM)

The main sally-port into Sumter, showing the confusion of rubble and the damage done by Beauregard's cannon. (NYHS)

Another view, April 17 or later, showing the effects of the fire from Charleston upon the mortar and masonry of the fort. (USAMHI)

On April 17, 1861, and probably for two or three days thereafter, two special photographers visited not only Fort Sumter, but also all of the Confederate installations that fired against it. They were James M. Osborn and F. E. Durbec of "Osborn & Durbec's Photographic Mart" at 223 King Street in Charleston. They operated a rather extensive establishment, advertising their "Cheap Photographs! Cheap Ambrotypes! Cheap Daguerreotypes! Cheap Ivorytypes! Cheap Melainotypes!"

and advised that strangers visiting Charleston "would do well to give us a call before going elsewhere." They sold views of Egypt, photo cases in some five thousand different patterns, and even carried cameras for sale. They are today forgotten, but on those days in April 1861 they took a place beside Brady and Gardner and Edwards and the rest of the war's immortal chroniclers.

Their stereo camera captured over forty scenes in Sumter and the Charleston batteries, the most

The only known photograph of the interior of Sumter's casemate, and the guns that Doubleday, Crawford, and others manned in defense. (TU)

complete record ever made of the site of a Civil War engagement. Apparently they later attempted to market their stereo views, but the war and the Federal blockade probably prevented their ever getting sufficient chemicals and supplies to manufacture the prints. As a result, very few of their images survive in more than one copy, and all but a few have been entirely lost to view until now.

What follows—in addition to the Osborn & Durbec views already presented in this and the previous chapter—is a nearly complete collection of their work. Two-thirds of these images have never before been published and are newly discovered.

As for Osborn & Durbec, their partnership did not survive the war. By 1866 they had gone their separate ways. They left behind a priceless record of the first sad evidence of war between the states.

A group of Confederate dignitaries in front of the shot furnace on Sumter's parade ground. Beside them is one of the columbiads that Anderson mounted to use as mortars against Charleston. They were never fired. The tall figure in the center has long been believed to be Wade Hampton. Others probably include Governor Francis Pickens. (TU)

The sally-port at Fort Sumter seen from the wharf. Already the conquering
Confederates are at work cleaning out the rubble and rebuilding. (TU)

The southwest face of the fort, showing the damage done by Edmund Ruffin
and members of his Palmetto Guard as they fired the columbiads in the Iron
Clad Battery. (CHS)

Damage done by Confederate guns firing from Cumming's Point. (TU)

The southwest corner, and the effects of shots fired from Morris Island and the Floating Battery. The opening at left is an embrasure for one of Sumter's guns. (CHS)

The southeast side of the parade, the hot-shot furnace, and the soldiers' east barracks. (CHS)

The ruins of the sally-port at right, and to its left the officers' quarters. (CHS)

Cleaning up the parade ground in front of the sally-port. (MHS)

The ruined officers' quarters on the southwest side, and a row of cannon Anderson did not emplace. (CHS)

The stair tower at an angle in the perimeter, and jaunty Confederates atop their captured guns. (TU)

Damage done by the Iron Clad Battery on the interior of Sumter. (CHS)

*In the left rear, the powder magazine, protected by an earth traverse. It is on
the side facing Charleston, since Sumter was built to withstand an attack from
the sea, not the land face.* (TU)

*Behind the makeshift flagstaff can be seen the effects of Fort Moultrie's fire on
the officers' quarters and sally-port.* (NA, BRADY COLLECTION)

The shot furnace and, to the right, Anderson's flagstaff, which was shot off during the bombardment. The new flag of the victors flutters overhead. (CHS)

More of the cleanup, with two men working while the others watch. (TU)

Sumter's parapet. Fort Moultrie is in the distance, while the guns shown are trained on the Iron Clad Battery. The gun in the foreground has been dismounted by Confederate fire. (CHS)

The rear of the same parapet, another dismounted gun, and a traverse built of sand bags to protect men from the fire from Sullivan's Island. (CWTI)

Confederates on Morris Island, very probably men of Colonel J. H. Trapier's Mortar Battery. (SOUTH CAROLINA HISTORICAL SOCIETY)

The Trapier Mortar Battery on Morris Island and, in the right background, Osborn & Durbec's pyramidal portable darkroom. (TU)

*Another view of the Trapier Battery, this time manned for action. At the very
right of the image, behind the dimly seen man at the edge, is a corner of the
portable darkroom.* (CHS)

*A view of the Iron Clad Battery at Morris
Island from the rear. The railroad "T"
iron cladding has been removed from its
wooden beamed roof. One of the
columbiads with which Ruffin sent the
first shots against Sumter can be seen
within.* (SOUTH CAROLINA HISTORICAL
SOCIETY)

The harbor face of Fort Moultrie, its shot furnace in the foreground. Since it was assumed that any attacker would come from the sea in wooden ships, the U. S. Army, when building these coastal forts, provided for sending red-hot shot like fireballs into attacking vessels. Just above the gun at the right can be seen a long dark object. It is Fort Sumter. These guns no longer bear upon it. (TU)

Another view of Moultrie's shot furnace, with the officers' quarters behind it. Heated shot from here set ablaze the wooden roofs in Sumter and caused fires that threatened the powder magazine. (TU)

The eastern angle of Moultrie, on Sullivan's Island. Damage done by Sumter's return fire can be seen in the roof of the right wing of the large house. (TU)

Moultrie's northwestern angle. (TU)

Moultrie's western barracks overlooking the parade ground, and the damage done by Captain Doubleday. (TU)

More of Doubleday's handiwork on the western barracks. It was small recompense. (TU)

A house on Sullivan's Island riddled by Surgeon Crawford's shot as he fired on the Floating Battery (TU)

Empty gun emplacements on Sullivan's Island and, in the harbor beyond, Fort Sumter. The bloodless beginning to a bloody war. (TU)

The Boys of '61

BELL I. WILEY

Euphoric thousands enlist before they miss "the fun"

THE TREMENDOUS WAVE of patriotism that swept over North and South in the wake of Fort Sumter produced an epidemic of volunteering. Very few of the recruits had any prior military experience. Conversion of the hordes of civilians into effective soldiers presented an enormous challenge, but authorities on both sides rose to the occasion and the results proved better than might have been expected.

Since governors usually took the lead in mobilization, most recruits had a brief stint of state service before they were sworn in as Federal or Confederate troops. First came a physical examination, usually a perfunctory test consisting largely of responses to questions put by the doctors concerning the recruits' medical history. Then came formal muster into national service—inspection by the muster officer, pledging allegiance to the United States or the Confederacy, promising to obey orders, swearing to abide by the 101 articles of war to which recruits listened while standing in company formation, and signing the company muster roll.

On both sides recruits chose their officers. As a rule the rank and file elected only their company officers (lieutenants and captains), who in turn chose the field grade officers (majors, lieutenant colonels, and colonels), but in some units soldiers elected all officers, from corporals to colonels. Those who took the lead in raising units were generally chosen to command them, but when, as was sometimes the case, more than one candidate vied for a position, lively campaigns ensued. Victors in these contests sometimes celebrated their success by hosting drinking parties.

During the first weeks in camp, recruits within the various companies organized themselves into informal groups known as messes. These varied in size from six to a dozen men, drawn together by similarity of inclination and interest. Members took turns in drawing rations, gathering wood, and cooking. Ties became very close with continuing association. An Illinois soldier wrote early in 1862: "Cap wanted to take some more men in our mess but we told him we would rather not, we wanted mess No. one to remain as it was. . . . Ours . . . is the most intelligent mess in this Reg[iment], the best fellows, the bravest boys, can kill more Secesh & Eat more hard Crackers & stand more hard marching, waid deeper mud & do less grumbling than any other mess in the Northern army."

As the time approached for departure from home for "the seat of war," volunteers took part in a series of farewell activities. One of these was the

presentation of a flag by one of the feminine pa-
triots who had helped to make it. As the pretty
donor made the presentation, she delivered a
flowery speech, extolling cause and country and
calling on the recipients to protect the emblem
from the vile creatures who sought to defile it. The
officer receiving the colors, usually a colonel, responded in words glowing with patriotism and
pledging himself and his associates to defend the
banner with their lives.

On the day of departure friends and neighbors
gathered at the railway station or steamboat wharf

or some other place of rendezvous to bid the soldiers farewell. After a prayer by a local minister,
the recruits took their leave amid a chorus of
good-byes and best wishes. The volunteers joked
and laughed to mask their sadness, and loved ones
left behind did their best to fight back the tears
that filled their eyes.

The trip to the fighting zone, made sometimes
by train and sometimes by boat, was a boisterous
experience. Troops traveling by rail sometimes obtained better ventilation and visibility by knocking
holes in the sides of boxcars; many rode on top of

As Lincoln and Davis issued their calls for the boys of '61, the first to be ready were those already enrolled in the scores of active militia units in North and South. New York photographer Charles D. Fredericks turned his camera out his own studio window on July 4, 1860, to catch this resplendent unit at parade. The bearskins would soon disappear. (USAMHI)

*The Kentucky State Guard encampment at Louisville in August 1860 proved a
training ground for several future Confederate companies. Commander of the
Guard was Brigadier General Simon Bolivar Buckner, soon to be a trusted
commander of the Confederacy. This group, the Lexington Rifles, was raised
and captained by John Hunt Morgan. In the fall of 1861 he would lead them
into the rebellion, to become a part of his famed cavalry. For now they are
content to pose and drink and feast on watermelon.* (KHS)

the cars, despite the admonitions of the officers. Escape from home restraints and the prospect of new
and exciting experiences brought a holiday attitude. So did the hearty cheering of pretty girls who
greeted them along the way. Many volunteers
added to their joviality by taking generous swigs
from liquor bottles which they had slipped into
their baggage before taking leave of their loved
ones. The first casualties experienced by some units
came not from hostile bullets but from tipsy soldiers falling from trains. The congestion and filth
of some of the trains and boats that transported
soldiers were enough to provoke excessive drinking.
In March 1862 an Illinois Yank wrote home from
West Tennessee: "We was aboard the steamer

Memphis 8 or 9 days. We was in dirt, lice, shit,
grease & Hard crackers."

Arrival at the front, whether in Tennessee, Kentucky, Missouri, Maryland, or Virginia, brought a
change in the character of soldiering. During the
initial period of service when the men were near
their homes, discipline was lax and duties relatively
light. Recruits frequently called their superiors by
their first names or addressed them as "sarge" or
"cap." Leaves were easy to obtain, and officers and
men spent much of their time in nearby towns or
cities. But the proximity of the enemy and the certainty of combat gave serious and urgent purpose
to training. Recruits and their officers came under
the control of hard-bitten professionals like Jo-

Buckner's own unit, the Citizen Guard, and more bearskins. (KHS)

seph E. Johnston, Braxton Bragg, U. S. Grant, and George B. McClellan. These commanders knew that the novices flowing in from farms, shops, and factories had to undergo a swift and drastic transformation before they could win battles. And they set themselves to effecting the change with determination and vigor. Men who previously treated soldiering as a lark now complained of the hardness of their lot. "I don't believe God ever intended for one man to pen up another and keep him in this manner," wrote a Reb to his homefolks; he added, "Dam Old Abe and Old Jeff Davis. Dam the day I 'listed." Another Reb wrote from a camp near Richmond in May 1861, "A man may come here with as much devil in him as they please, but they will soon tame him." A Georgian, after his transfer to Virginia in the fall of 1861, wrote his father: "I love my country as well as any one but I don't believe in the plan of making myself a slave. . . . A private soldier is nothing more than a slave and is often treated worse. I have during the past six

months gone through more hardships than anyone of ours or Grandma's negroes; their life is a luxury to what mine is sometimes." But this soldier came to realize the value of discipline, and while he never completely gave up the cherished practice of grumbling, he eventually accepted and approved the new order. The same was true of most of his comrades and of the men they fought.

In the fighting zones, platoons, companies, and regiments had to be fitted into larger organizations. Two platoons, each commanded by a lieutenant, comprised a company, led by a captain; ten companies formed a regiment, commanded by a colonel; two or more regiments comprised a brigade, led by a brigadier general; two or more brigades combined to make a division, commanded by a major general; two or more divisions comprised a corps, commanded by a lieutenant general on the Confederate side and a major general on the Union side; and two or more corps made an army, commanded by a full general on the Confederate

But militia were not enough. New volunteer armies must be raised. Though defeated by Lincoln in 1860, Stephen A. Douglas stood firmly behind his antagonist's administration, and now took to the stump in speaking to raise support and volunteers. He wore himself out in the process, and died that summer. The last words of his final public address declared his stand for the Union: "United, firm, determined, never to permit the Government to be destroyed." (USAMHI)

thing over one hundred officers and men. But, after the first few months of service, companies commonly dwindled to about half their authorized strength and subsequently some experienced even greater attrition. Long and intimate association and the sharing of perils and hardships of soldiering promoted a relationship among company officers and their men very much like that of a family. The captain was the father who supervised daily routine, saw that his men were equipped, fed, clothed, and sheltered, heard their complaints, administered punishment for minor offenses, looked after their health, and led them in combat. He knew every man by name and had some acquaintance with the soldier's home circumstances. He sometimes mediated domestic squabbles, wrote letters for illiterates, supervised religious worship, buried the dead, and wrote letters of sympathy to bereaved wives and mothers. The lieutenants and noncommissioned officers were the captain's helpers and their role was very much like that of the elder children in a large family. A key member of the group was the company's first or orderly sergeant, who called the roll, kept the records, and translated the captain's wishes into orders.

On the Confederate side, and to an increasing

Lincoln's old friend Senator Edward Baker of Oregon helped raise a regiment. He would lead it to destruction, and his own death, at Ball's Bluff in October. (RICHARD C. OSTERHOUT)

side and a major general on the Union side. In the artillery, the battalion, consisting of four batteries, each containing four to six guns, was a standard organization. The squadron (known also as the troop and the equivalent roughly of the infantry company) consisting of two or more platoons was a distinctive feature of the cavalry organization. Combination of arms normally began with the attachment of artillery (usually a battery) and cavalry to an infantry brigade. Engineer, signal, and other supporting elements were added on the corps or army level.

The basic unit on both sides was the infantry company, which at full strength numbered some-extent among the Federals, blacks were obtained to help clean quarters, launder clothing, clean boots and shoes, cook, and perform other menial chores. Early in the war some enlisted men even had one or more Negroes, usually body servants, to lighten the burdens of camp life, even to the extent of standing guard under the supervision of their masters. But after a few months most of these servants went home; those who remained were usually the personal aides of officers, or blacks assigned to companies and regiments as hostlers or teamsters. The blacks encountered in northern camps were ex-slaves hired for a pittance to relieve officers and men of some of the more burdensome aspects of army service. Home letters of many Yanks in 1861 and later told of the writer's good fortune in having obtained the service of black menials. Private Andrew Rose of an Ohio regiment stationed in middle Tennessee wrote his parents in 1863: "The captain got two nigers for our company; every company has got them; all we do when we want nigers is to send a company after them." In 1862 a Maine captain wrote from Louisiana: "Officers & men are having an easy time. We have Negroes to do all fatigue work, cooking and washing clothes." In both armies black servants were often called on to dance and provide music for the entertainment of officers and soldiers. The Negroes sometimes sought diversion for themselves by gambling and drinking. During the last two years of the war, about 200,000 blacks were recruited by the Federals for service as soldiers. Inspection reports show that colored troops were often required to do more than their share of labor and that sometimes their white commander treated them more like menials than as fighters.

The training received by Johnny Reb and Billy Yank was very much alike. *Hardee's Tactics*—written by William J. Hardee, a Confederate general—was the most widely used infantry manual on both sides. In accordance with rules prescribed by Hardee for "the school of the soldier" recruits mastered such fundamentals as saluting or standing erect; facing left and right; marching forward, to the rear, by the flank, and obliquely; shifting arms to the various positions; parrying and thrusting with the bayonet; and loading and firing their guns standing, kneeling, and lying down. Most Yanks and Rebs were armed either with the Springfield or the Enfield rifled musket. Since both were muzzle-

Colonel E. Elmer Ellsworth, once a denizen of Lincoln's Illinois law office, brought his New York Fire Zouaves, composed chiefly of New York City firemen, to Washington soon after the crisis came to shots at Sumter. (NYHS)

loaders, much time and patience were required for their effective use. For loading the gun Hardee specified nine movements, each initiated by the instructor's command. At the order "Load!" the soldier dropped the butt of his gun to the ground, grasped the barrel with his left hand and with his right hand reached for the cartridge box hanging from his belt. In response to subsequent commands he bit the end from the paper cartridge; poured the powder into the barrel; inserted the bullet, with hollow base down, into the muzzle and with a ramrod pushed it to the other end of the barrel; returned the ramrod to its place beneath the barrel;

took a percussion cap from a leather pouch on his belt and placed it on the nipple of the tube extending from beneath the hammer into the barrel; and shifted the gun to his right shoulder. Firing was then accomplished by movements executed at the commands "Ready," "Aim," "Fire." Despite the complexity of the procedure, a well-trained infantryman could load and fire his gun twice a minute.

After obtaining proficiency in the use of their rifles, soldiers were taught progressively to march and maneuver in squads, companies, regiments, brigades, and divisions. However, drills by units larger than brigades were infrequent and "sham battles," with infantry, artillery, and cavalry functioning together, were almost unknown until after the first year of the war, and even then they were rare.

Other branches followed a training routine comparable to that of the infantry. In the artillery much practice was required for each member of the gun crew to become proficient in his duties; the most widely used field piece on both sides was the 12-pounder smoothbore called the Napoleon. Functioning by numbers, from 1 to 10, each crew-

man not only had to make the specific movement associated with his number, such as removing the shell from the ammunition chest, passing it on to another, placing it in the muzzle, and ramming it down, but he also had to learn the movements assigned to all the other numbers so that when casualties were experienced shifts could be made without loss of efficiency.

While learning to drill and to use their weapons, recruits had to adjust to the regimented routine of army life. The soldier's day was ordered by drum or bugle calls, which ordinarily ran to about a dozen. First came reveille, sounded about dawn, to wake the soldiers and summon them to roll call. After lining up and responding to their names, they were dismissed until a second call a half-hour later ordered them to breakfast. The third call sent the ailing to the regimental surgeon and the well to such duties as cleaning quarters, tidying company grounds, and cutting wood. About eight o'clock, the musicians sounded the call for guard mounting, at which the first sergeant of each company turned out his guard detail for the next twenty-four hours' duty, inspected them, and marched them to the regimental parade ground. There the guards were

To the War Department in Washington fell the task of organizing, equipping, training, and assigning the largest army ever raised in the hemisphere. No one had any experience in dealing with such numbers. (CHS)

formed into line, inspected by the adjutant, and sent to their respective posts. Details were so arranged that each member stood guard only two hours out of every six.

Next came the call for drill, which ordinarily lasted until drummer or bugler signaled "roast beef," which was the call for lunch. Following a brief post-luncheon period of relaxation, soldiers were summoned to another drill which normally lasted from one to two hours. Then the men returned to their quarters, brushed their uniforms, blacked their leather, polished buckles and buttons, and cleaned their weapons in preparation for retreat, which consisted of roll call, inspection, and dress parade. Both officers and men took pride in the dress parade, held sometimes by regiment and sometimes by brigade, and always to the accompaniment of music. Dress parades were the occasion for reading orders and making official announcements.

Supper call came shortly after retreat, followed not long after dark by tattoo, which brought another roll call, after which the men returned to their quarters. The final call of the day required the cessation of noise and the extinguishing of lights. In the course of the war this call became "taps."

This was the typical routine of an infantry regiment in camp during a season of quiet. Practices varied to some extent in different camps and with changing situations. Sunday routine differed from that of other days. The major event on the Sabbath was a general inspection of quarters, grounds, personnel, and equipment. After a preliminary check by the units' own officers, the regiment or battalion formed by companies. The inspector, usually the brigade commander or one of his staff, proceeded up and down the open ranks, carefully observing clothing, weapons, and other equipment. The soldiers were then required to stack arms, unsling and open their knapsacks, and lay them on the ground for examination. The inspector checked the contents of the knapsacks, and if he found a dirty garment he rebuked the offender. Further reproof for this and any other faults discovered by the inspector was given by the unit commander after the men returned to their quarters. The inspecting officer made the rounds of guardhouse, hospital, sutler's shop, kitchen, and such other facilities as he chose to examine. He concluded the

Officers like Brigadier General George Cadwallader did their best to hold precarious states like Maryland and Kentucky in the Union when Lincoln's call for volunteers to put down the rebellion aroused their southern sympathies. Cadwallader defied Chief Justice Roger B. Taney himself in carrying out Lincoln's suspension of the writ of habeas corpus in Maryland, for fear of seeing it secede. (USAMHI)

inspection shortly before noon by going through the company quarters and checking floors, bunks, and walls. Soldiers usually spent Sunday afternoons writing letters, playing games, reading, or gambling. Those of religious inclination might attend prayer meetings or listen to sermons delivered by the regimental chaplain or by one of their comrades.

Every other month soldiers were mustered for pay. Standing in company formation, each soldier certified his presence by responding "here" when his name was called. After the mustering officer

The courthouse at Natchez, Mississippi, long thought to show Confederates enlisting in 1861. The photo, by Henry Gurney, more likely depicts Federal soldiers sometime after 1862, but the scene would be much the same if they were wearers of the gray. (JOAN AND THOMAS GANDY)

had accounted for every man listed on the roster, he forwarded a copy of the muster roll to the adjutant general in Washington, or Richmond. At the beginning of the war the monthly pay on both sides was $11 for infantry and artillery privates and $12 for cavalry. Early in the conflict the Union government increased the pay of privates in all three branches to $13 a month and in May 1864 to $16. Confederates received only one raise and that was on June 9, 1864, when the monthly stipend of infantry and artillery privates was increased to $20 and that of cavalry privates to $21; by that time the gold value of the Confederate dollar had shrunk to about five cents. Pay was often in arrears, sometimes as much as four months on the Union side and six to twelve months among Confederates.

An essential part of the transition from civilian to soldier was getting accustomed to military clothing. On both sides the first uniforms worn by some soldiers were those in which they had paraded as

militiamen. These varied considerably in color and design. Concerning troops whom he observed in Washington in the early summer of 1861, General William T. Sherman stated: "Their uniforms were as various as the cities and states from which they came." When Northerners wore gray militia uniforms into battle and Southerners wore blue, as was the case in some of the early engagements, they had the unhappy experience of being fired on by their comrades. In 1861 and later, both sides had some Zouave units that wore fezzes, red bloomers, gaily colored vests and sashes, and white gaiters. Considerable variation in dress persisted throughout the war, but a fair degree of standardization was achieved in both armies before the end of 1861.

The usual outfit of a Federal infantryman was a long woolen dress coat of dark blue with a high stiff collar; a dark blue jacket or blouse which for field service was much preferred to the dress coat; light blue trousers; black brogan shoes; a flannel shirt; long flannel drawers; socks; blue cap with black visor; and a long blue overcoat with cape. Artillery and cavalry dress was the same as for the infantry except the coats were shorter and boots were normally worn instead of shoes. In both armies each branch had distinctive trimmings (red for artillery, blue for infantry, and yellow for cavalry). Branch was also indicated by insignia worn on the front of the headgear; Union officers below the grade of generals wore crossed cannons for artillery, a bugle for infantry, crossed sabers for cavalry, turreted castle for engineers, and flaming shell for ordnance, along with a brass numeral designating regiment and, when applicable, a brass letter specifying company. Union privates wore brass letters and numerals on their caps to indicate company and regiment; on the Confederate side, branch was designated by the color of the cap crown.

Confederate Army regulations specified a double-breasted coat for both officers and enlisted men, but among enlisted men this garment was rarely seen after the first few months of the conflict. In its stead a short, gray single-breasted jacket was worn, thus giving to Johnny Rebs the nickname "gray jackets." Confederate Army regulations also specified trousers of dark blue, but from the beginning, until the use of homemade dyes produced a yellowish brown or "butternut" hue, trousers, like coats, were of gray. Confederate shoes and socks at first were very much like those worn by Yanks, but after the northern blockade became effective, inferior shoes made of home-tanned leather had to be used, though many Rebs equipped themselves with sturdier footwear by appropriating the shoes of Yankee battle casualties. Some Confederates, especially those of rural background, regarded drawers as superfluous. Regulations of both armies listed leather stocks or ties as standard items of issue, but these were rarely worn. Many soldiers in both armies wore soft hats instead of caps. Well-meaning relatives North and South frequently loaded the soldiers down with "extras" such as havelocks to protect necks from sun and rain, sleeping caps, scarfs, and mittens, but these were usually discarded soon after the recruits arrived in camp, if not before.

The soldier's prescribed equipment included a haversack for his food, a canteen, a knapsack for extra items of clothing, stationery, toilet articles, and other personal items, a leather cartridge box, and a small leather pouch for percussion caps. But comfort, convenience, and other considerations led to a shedding of some of this equipment. Knapsacks were frequently discarded and the contents rolled in a blanket which the soldier threw over his left shoulder and tied at the ends above his right hip. Many Rebs and Yanks regarded tin cups and small skillets as essential items of equipment. These they suspended from their belts. The cups sometimes were used for boiling coffee over the coals of the campfire.

During their period of breaking in as soldiers, Yanks and Rebs frequently had to sleep on the ground under the open skies. Those fortunate enough to have shelter usually were occupants of either Sibley or "A" tents. The Sibley tent, shaped like a bell or wigwam and supported by a vertical center pole, was eighteen feet in diameter and twelve feet high. Its twelve or more occupants slept with their feet to the center and heads near the outer edge, like spokes in a wheel. Guns were stacked around the center pole and other equipment arranged according to comfort and convenience. "A" tents, known also as wedge tents, consisted of a large sheet of canvas draped over a long horizontal bar supported by upright poles, placed at each end. Front and rear were covered by two other pieces of canvas which, when tied together, had the shape of an "A." Each tent housed from four to six men; occupants could stand upright only when directly beneath the center ridge-pole, and in sleeping they found maximum comfort when arranged in spoon fashion; but this meant that when one turned over, all had to do likewise. Officers normally were housed in wall tents, which, in effect, were "A" tents elevated two to four feet from the ground and walled with canvas. They were much more commodious and comfortable for their one or two occupants than were the Sibley and wedge tents.

After 1861 Sibley and "A" tents generally were replaced by lighter and less expensive dwellings known as shelter tents, or dog tents. These were two-man habitations made by buttoning together the rectangular pieces of canvas known as half shelters which each soldier carried as a part of his equipment. These halves, when combined, were made into a miniature wedge, with both ends open. Sometimes four soldiers would combine their

A recruiting scene in an unidentified town. These men, perhaps, are Confederates. Certainly they have the rugged look of those rough-edged, tough men of the trans-Appalachian west who, North and South, proved to be the fiercest fighters—and worst disciplined—of the war. (JMB)

half shelters to make a larger covering. Lacking a partner, a soldier could stretch his half shelter horizontally over a framework of four horizontal sticks, one placed at each corner. Ingenious Rebs and Yanks arranged their shelters in various other ways to satisfy their tastes and comforts.

In seasons of cold, when the military situation was quiescent, soldiers winterized their tents or built log cabins. A winterized tent was a rectangular log pen, about four feet high, roofed with sloping canvas and with the interior dug out perhaps to a depth of two feet to provide more standing room and warmth. Log cabins were one-room huts, chinked and daubed like frontier dwellings. Roofs were of boards, grass, or canvas. Spaciousness of the huts was sometimes increased by digging out the interiors. Both huts and winterized tents were heated by fireplaces with chimneys built of logs and chinked and lined with clay. Often chimneys were topped with barrels or kegs to increase the draft, provide better combustion, and keep the dwellings free of smoke. Sometimes chimneys would catch fire and cause a great commotion in the soldier community.

Many soldiers laid wooden floors to increase the comfort of their winter residences. They drove nails or pegs around the walls for the hanging of hats, haversacks, and cartridge boxes. They made stoves and tables of boxes or barrels obtained from the commissary or of boards taken from nearby barns or residences. Some built double- or triple-deck bunks along the walls to converse space. Bayonets were stuck into floors or walls and candles inserted in the sockets to provide illumination. Photographs, books, and writing materials were conveniently arranged on shelves and tables. Some soldiers added a humorous touch by placarding the entrance of their huts with designations such as "Buzzard Roost," "Astor House," "Howlers," and "Growlers." Many Yanks and Rebs boasted to their womenfolk about the comfort and attractiveness of their winter quarters. A Texan stationed in Virginia wrote his mother on January 14, 1862: "Our house is about 12 feet square. . . . Our guns are in racks on the walls; our utensils consist of one skillet, a stew kettle, a bread pan, a frying pan, & a large kettle. Our china ware is a half dozen plates and the same number of forks & spoons (silver of

They came in whole families, like these four brothers in blue with their target rifles. (LO)

They spoke in strange tongues, like men of this all-German artillery unit. Tens of thousands of Germans marched behind the Federal banners, often induced to volunteer by high rank being given—sometimes unwisely—to prominent Germans. (AMERICANA IMAGE GALLERY)

They came in baggy pants, the uniform of the French Zouave. (USAMHI)

area. A New Englander stationed near Falls Church, Virginia, wrote his homefolks in January 1862: "The 2nd Maine have erected arches and other fancy works over the entrance to each avenue. These are made of cedar boughs and trees set in and around their camps. Nor has the 17th N. Y. been behind in beautifying their grounds. Over the entrance is placed the name of 'McClellan'—below and on the right is 'Porter' (commanding division), on the left Butterfield (commanding brigade)." Because of the comfort of their winter dwellings, and the respite from marching and fighting that came with cold weather, most soldiers came to regard winter as the most tolerable of their wartime seasons.

For many recruits the most undesirable feature of breaking in to army life was being "put through the measles." Troops from rural areas, largely because they had not been exposed to this malady in childhood, were more susceptible to it than were those from towns and cities. Measles usually struck during the first few months of military service and with devastating consequences. In the summer of 1861, one out of every seven Confederates of the Army of Northern Virginia had measles, and in one camp of 10,000 recruits, 4,000 men were stricken with the disease. Early in 1863 a soldier of Grant's army wrote from near Vicksburg: "Mesles . . . is what kilde the most of our boys—thay would take the measels and haf to lay out in the rain and storm and thay wod only laste abot 2 days." Comparatively few men died from measles alone, but the tendency to get up too soon often led to complications which proved fatal. A soldier of the Army of Northern Virginia wrote in August 1861: "We have some 5 or 6 that is very sick ones in our company. . . . They all had the measles, & were getting well & they turn out to drill too soon after it and they all have relapsed." Recruits of 1861 also had dysentery, malaria, typhoid, pneumonia, and other diseases that plagued Civil War armies, but the incidence of measles was much greater among new soldiers than among veterans.

Yet sickness, discomfort, drill, and discipline paled in comparison to the real business of soldiering, and all too soon these boys of '61 would mature in fire and blood to become the men of Bull Run.

course), our cups are of tin, 4 quart cups and two pint cups. Just above the fireplace you will see something which we call a mantle piece. . . . There are only four of us in this house." A member of the 16th Maine Regiment wrote from near Fredericksburg, Virginia, in January 1863: "Max and I built generously, and inside our finished house, in the warmth of a roaring blaze, we set up bedsteads and overlaid them with pine boughs for mattresses, and covered the boughs with blankets for counterpanes. How proudly we gazed upon those beds!"

Members of some regiments, after completing their huts, built ornate entrances to their camping

They came magnificently equipped, like Sergeant Dore of the 7th New York State Militia. (USAMHI)

They came, like Lieutenant A. Kintzing Post of the 45th Massachusetts, enlisting for and expecting a nine-month war. (USAMHI)

*And they came young. This unknown boy wears the fatigue blouse and cap, common dress for most Federal infantry. (*ROBERT MCDONALD*)*

*And younger still they came. A photograph taken in 1861 by Lieutenant Henry Digby of Ohio, of drummer boys William Ambrose and James C. Calias. (*AMERICANA IMAGE GALLERY*)*

*And still younger. David Wood, aged ten. The children came to be drummers, but many, the larger ones, often passed for beyond their years and took their place in the battle. The veterans sometimes sang nursery songs in camp when they spied these boys of '61. But it was a young man's war. Some "boys" would be generals before they were old enough to vote. (*RICHARD E. WOOD*)*

The Southrons flocked to their country's call, too. At Fredericksburg, Virginia, in June 1861, these confident young Virginians posed in a mixture of military and civilian dress. For many it was the best they would ever get. (JOHN A. HESS)

C. C. Taylor, J. D. Jackson, and a man named Porter, all from Georgia, enlisted in the 3d Georgia Infantry, but did not leave for war before posing for this ambrotype. The numbers were against them. In this war, nearly one of every three Confederates would die. (MC)

Two brothers in gray. Very quickly the Confederate soldier would learn to supply his own needs from what he might capture from the enemy. For these two that meant United States Army belt plates. (HP)

They came to photographers who supplied them with props like Roman short
swords and sometimes ungrammatical patriotic expressions. Musician Private
Joseph C. White of the 12th Mississippi, with the props that the photographer
used with a number of Confederates. (FRANK R. JOHNSON)

They came with boyish bravado and clowning. (WILLIAM A. ALBAUGH)

They came with double-barreled shotguns, huge bowie knives, and a look of wild determination. (HP)

Some looked rather bemused by it all. (WILLIAM A. ALBAUGH)

They came looking ready and alert, like Henry Kelley of the 1st Virginia, with his Colt revolving rifle. (RONN PALM)

And they came without spit or polish or posture. (LES JENSEN)

They came with poise and dignity, obviously the sons of the first families. (WENDELL W. LANG, JR.)

And they, too, came young. Brother privates, William E. Spach and Bennett Spach, of the 1st Battalion of North Carolina Sharpshooters. (JOHN T. SPACH)

North and South, the departure of the volunteers for the front was a major occasion. With great ceremony the town fathers or state officials presented the regiments with their colors. Here the 1st Michigan Infantry receive their flags in Detroit on May 1, 1861. (BURTON HISTORICAL COLLECTION, DETROIT PUBLIC LIBRARY)

Then it was off to the war. In April 1861, the 1st Rhode Island Infantry marched to the railroad depot in Providence to ride to the South, their governor, William Sprague, at their head. (RHODE ISLAND HISTORICAL SOCIETY)

Camps of instruction like Camp Chase outside Washington appeared all over the divided nation, as volunteers poured in to be made into soldiers. (OHIO HISTORICAL SOCIETY)

Hasty makeshift bivouacs sprang forth in most major cities, crowding even major public buildings and filling the square in front of Philadelphia's Independence Hall. (LO)

"*I have seen Him in the watch-fires of a hundred circling camps,*" *wrote Julia Ward Howe. The camp of the 1st Connecticut Artillery, near Washington.* (CHS)

The 7th New York State Militia on review in 1861 at Camp Cameron. The drill and review were all too new to the recruits of 1861. It would become all too familiar in the years to come. (MHS)

The 9th Mississippi on parade near Pensacola, caught by J. D. Edwards in April 1861. They, too, however rustic in appearance, learned the intricacies of the drill manual, though it often baffled them. They fought back by giving to the evolutions their own peculiar appellations. A right wheel soon became a "stauchendicilar to the right." (MC)

Men of the 5th Company, Washington Artillery of New Orleans, at Camp Lewis, near Carrolton, Louisiana. This new camp life was for them, as for their Yankee counterparts, a lark in the days when the war was young and bound only to last a few months. A photograph by J. W. Petty of New Orleans. (CM)

The soldiers read, relaxed, played cards, tickled each other in the ear with feathers, and even stacked the deck for the camera. The gambler to the left holds a "full house," kings and twos. Even a passing bird stops to perch on the cannon's sponge for the photographer. The 1st Massachusetts Light Artillery. (USAMHI)

Many Confederates, even private soldiers, appeared for muster with their bodyservants in tow. Andrew Chandler brought his slave Silas Chandler with him, and both armed for a fight. Men who once feared arms in the hands of slaves now thought little of handing them knives and shotguns. (STERLING CHANDLER AND RICHARD S. YOUNG)

Yankees, too, enjoyed the services of blacks when they could get them. Here is the little servant of Captain Aspinwall of the 22d New York. (USAMHI)

*Most of all the men North and South did as American soldiers have done in all
wars, make the best of it. Confederates of the Washington Artillery relaxed,
indifferent to what lay ahead. When they left New Orleans they were told,
"May the Lord of Hosts be round about you as a wall of fire, and shield your
heads in the day of battle!"* (JAN P. REIFENBERG)

They and their foes to the north, like the 7th New York, will be ready, or think they will. None of them, in their bright uniforms . . . (USAMHI)

. . . their gaily festooned quarters for "Phunny Fellows" . . . (USAMHI)

. . . their striped trousers, their blouses decorated with flannel badges and galloping horses . . . (USAMHI)

. . . none of them, for all their pretended preparedness, really know what is coming. (USAMHI)

Instead, they smile and pose. The 23d New York Infantry. (USAMHI)

They pose in little groups. The 33d New York Infantry, the man at right armed with a "Volcanic" repeating pistol in his belt. (USAMHI)

They pose by companies, their lady friends often with them. The 22d New York State Militia. (USAMHI)

*They gather around the colors they expect to lead to glory, and defend with
their lives if need be. The colors of the 7th New York State Militia, at right and
left the general guides, at left center the regimental banner, and right center the
national colors.* (NA)

The officers and men join together for the camera. Colonel William Wilson, center, and men of his 6th New York Infantry, "Wilson's Zouaves." (USAMHI)

They clowned indoors at mock battle. (LO)

With bread and cider and camaraderie, they passed the summer days of soldiering. But it would not last. These militiamen are guarding the Chain Bridge over the Potomac at Washington in 1861. (RINHART GALLERIES INC.)

*Washington was a threatened capital. With
Virginia across the Potomac hostile, and Maryland
filled with southern sympathizers who attempted to
block Federal communications and reinforcement
from the North, Lincoln and his city were almost
blockaded. Then Benjamin F. Butler, a
Massachusetts Democrat and now an ardent
supporter of the war, acted under his major
general's commission and led an expedition to
secure . . .* (MICHAEL J. MCAFEE)

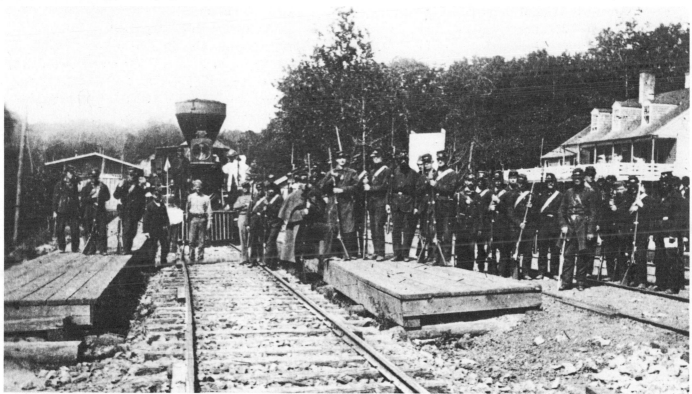

*. . . the Baltimore & Ohio Railroad junction at Relay House, Maryland, thereby
holding open a rail route for troops to reach Washington. From May 6, 1861,
onward, troops like these flowed through Relay House and on to the capital.*
(MHS)

The First Bull Run

JOSEPH P. CULLEN

Reality at last in the heat and dust and blood of Manassas

IT WAS ALREADY HOT that morning of July 16, 1861, when they marched out of the camps around Washington to fight the first major battle in what has been called the last of the old wars and the first of the new. And the camera would be there, or not far behind, to record for posterity the men of the armies and the scenes of battle—a hill, a stream, a field, a copse of woods; a bridge, a church, a house, a barn. Ordinary everyday things in ordinary, everyday life, but these simple things assumed importance beyond their functional purposes. They became landmarks to show where men fought and died; landmarks to be photographed and recorded for future generations.

Since April, when the guns of Fort Sumter roared out their message that North and South were at war, troops had poured into the Washington area until the surrounding heights blossomed white with tents in a care-free, carnival atmosphere. And the untrained, undisciplined citizen-soldiers, with their gaudy, multicolored uniforms—the flamboyant 11th New York Zouaves in their blue and scarlet shirts and jackets and white turbans; the checked flannels of Michigan lumberjacks; the colorful Garibaldi Guards—added a picturesque touch. A few were army regulars, some state militia, but most were three-month volunteers

with romantic ideas about wars in general and battles in particular, who fully expected to end the war with one battle and be home at the end of their brief enlistment.

Many tried to bring the comforts of home with them into the field. One volunteer admitted that his knapsack held "a pair of trousers, two pairs of drawers, a pair of thick boots, four pairs of stockings, four flannel shirts, a blouse, a looking glass, a can of peaches, a bottle of cough-mixture, a button-stick, chalk, razor and strop, a Bible, a small volume of Shakespere, and writing utensils," in addition to a "tailor's shop," usually made of leather or cloth and "containing needles, pins, thread, buttons, and scissors." He also carried a rubber blanket and a woolen blanket and "a belt bout the body, which held a cartridge-box and bayonet, a cross-belt, also a haversack and tin drinking cup, a canteen." The cartridge-box held forty rounds of ammunition and the haversack three days' rations of "salt junk, hardtack, sugar and coffee." Altogether a load to challenge a mule.

There was an air of excitement, a feeling akin to a sudden unexpected holiday, a welcome break in the humdrum monotony of everyday living. And that feeling was very much in evidence that morning as 35,000 men in their colorful uniforms, carrying the stiff new flags clinging to their shiny staffs, marched off to battle with bands blaring and drums rolling. They knew nothing of wars or battles or any of the realities of actual combat. They expected to march for a few days and then line up somewhere in formation and shoot at the enemy from afar. Then when the Southerners ran back to Richmond it would be over and they could all go home as heroes. So they went to war as if to a picnic.

After a few days of marching in the brutal heat and choking dust, however, many of these civilian-soldiers began to have second thoughts about the glorious adventure ahead of them. "My canteen banged against my bayonet," one recruit noted, "both tin cup and bayonet badly interfered with the butt of my musket, while my cartridge-box and haversack were constantly flopping up and down." Blistered feet and aching muscles soon dictated that loads had to be lightened, so various pieces of equipment were surreptitiously dropped along the way. Thus would they learn the hard way—by experience.

In command of this ragged mass of men marching out of Washington was Irvin McDowell, a native of Ohio recently promoted to brigadier general of volunteers. A graduate of the U. S. Military Academy, McDowell was forty-three years old, a robust, heavy-set man with dark cropped hair and an iron-gray beard. He had served creditably in the Mexican War in staff positions, but had never commanded a large body of troops in the field. A quiet, introverted person who neither smoked nor drank, he was too reserved to be popular with his fellow officers, and definitely not the type to inspire men. Still he was a professional and as such recognized the weaknesses of his raw recruits. He did not want to fight until the men had been trained sufficiently to at least act like soldiers rather than civilians. "This is not an army," he told his superiors. "It will take a long time to make an army." But the times were against McDowell. The enlistments of most of the three-month volunteers was about up and the people of the North became impatient. "Forward to Richmond" screamed the newspaper headlines. And the government listened to the voice of the people. McDowell was ordered to move against a lesser Confederate force at Manassas, Virginia, about twenty-five miles southwest of Washington. To be sure, there was another

Confederate force to the west in the Shenandoah Valley, but it was to be pinned down by other Federal troops and thus prevented from reinforcing the Confederates at Manassas. "You are green, it is true," President Lincoln told the reluctant McDowell, "but they are green also."

And green they were. A few days after the firing at Fort Sumter, Virginia seceded from the Union. In Richmond there was dancing in the streets and bonfires burned to celebrate the historic event. Cannon were dragged by hand from the state arsenal to Capitol Square to fire a salute. The new Confederate flag fluttered proudly atop the capitol building. Virginians by the thousands flocked to the newly opened recruiting stations, fearful the fighting would end before they could play a part in it. Then in May the Confederate Congress, in session at Montgomery, Alabama, voted to move the Confederate capital to Richmond. Now the city underwent a dramatic change. When hundreds of regiments from farther south streamed in, Richmond took on the appearance of a vast military camp. At night the glow from thousands of campfires lit the sky. One observer noted, "One of the remarkable features of the times is that men of all classes and conditions, of all occupations and professions, are of one mind."

Although a Richmond newspaper could bluster, "There is one wild shout of fierce resolve to capture Washington City, at all and every human hazard," that was not the immediate objective of the new government. If the South could not secede from the Union peacefully, then it was determined to defend every acre of territory and maintain its independence to the last. As Confederate President Davis proclaimed: "All we ask is to be left alone." With this philosophy there was nothing to be gained by invading the North. Rather, the South wanted to exploit the advantages of a defensive posture, which would require fewer men and allow it to use its interior, or shorter, lines of communications and supply to best advantage. In addition, all the various government departments, as well as an army, had to be created, organized, and staffed to carry on a war, while at the same time a government had to be set up to pass laws governing what was hoped would be a new nation.

So thousands of young men streamed into Richmond to prepare to defend their independence, and like their counterparts in Washington, their uniforms exhibited an amazing variety. The various state militia colors mixed with fancy home-made uniforms, while some regiments had nothing but civilian clothes. Some of the higher ranking officers still wore the dress of the United States Army. And like the Northerners, the new recruits posed stiffly for portraits, followed the bands down the springtime streets, waved to the cheering girls, and set about, they thought, getting the war over with in a hurry. As one lady recorded in her diary, "There was much music and mustering and marching, much cheering and flying of flags, much firing of guns and all that sort of thing."

With Richmond now the Confederate capital, the area of Manassas, about seventy-five miles to the north, became strategically important to the defense of the city. The central point was Manassas Junction, a small railroad settlement consisting of a handful of decrepit buildings scattered carelessly about the railroad crossing. Here two railroads joined. The Orange & Alexandria, running north and south, connected with both Washington and Richmond; and the Manassas Gap Railroad, which extended westward through the Blue Ridge mountains to the rich, fertile valley of the Shenandoah. There were many good roads also, east and west, north and south, the main one being the Warrenton Turnpike, which led through the town of Centreville to Alexandria and Washington. The surrounding area was a gently rolling country of soft ridges, small farms, rail fences, crooked creeks, and quiet woods. About midway between Manassas and Centreville, Bull Run Creek meandered peacefully through the plains, the trees along its banks forming a leafy tunnel with the sun sifting through to form lacy gold patterns on the water, while picturesque arched bridges spanned it.

In June the South moved to protect this vital point. In command was Brigadier General P. G. T. Beauregard, hero of the firing on Fort Sumter. A

In the wake of Fort Sumter, the pressure on Lieutenant General Winfield Scott—shown here with his staff—became intense. The Union must strike back, put down the Rebellion. (NA)

First Washington must be made secure and troops brought in from the North.
Benjamin F. Butler's occupation of Relay House on the vital Baltimore & Ohio
ensured that (USAMIII)

classmate of McDowell's, his last United States Army assignment had been as Superintendent of the Military Academy at West Point, New York. A small, graceful man in his early forties, Beauregard was a proud Creole from Louisiana who had distinguished himself in the Mexican War as a staff officer but, like McDowell, had never commanded a large body of troops in the field. Outspoken and critical of others, yet sensitive to criticism himself, he generally found it easier to make enemies than friends. But he too was a professional, and now with about 22,000 raw civilian-soldiers he set his line of defense along Bull Run. Although the creek itself was a formidable obstacle to any attacking force with its steep wooded banks, there were many fords and two bridges to be defended. On his right flank he destroyed the railroad bridge at Union Mills; built fortifications at McLean's, Blackburn's,

and Mitchell's fords; and stationed other forces at Ball's Ford, Lewis Ford, and the Stone Bridge on the Warrenton Turnpike, his extreme left flank. At Manassas Junction itself massive fortifications were erected running out in different directions from the little station. And across Bull Run he established advance guard posts at Centreville and Fairfax Court House and several strategic crossroads to warn of the approach of the enemy. Sixty miles away to the west across the mountains sat another force under Brigadier General Joseph E. Johnston. If Beauregard was outnumbered and attacked, he hoped to be reinforced by Johnston's troops. They would come on the cars of the Manassas Gap Railroad.

While these preparations were being made, the recruits were constantly marshaled and drilled in a desperate attempt to give them some training be-

With men of the 7th New York and other regiments garrisoning the camps around Washington, the capital was safe. That done, it was time to press the war and end the Rebellion. Within weeks these boys of '61 would become men in battle. (WRHS)

behind Bull Run. McDowell spent the next two days probing for a weak spot in the Confederate line. A reconnaissance in force was repulsed in the center at Mitchell's and Blackburn's fords, and no suitable terrain for attack appeared on the right. On the Confederate left, however, two unguarded fords, Popular and Sudley, were discovered. A crossing here would put the troops on the Sudley road, which led to the Warrenton Turnpike near the Stone House, and behind the Confederate left.

So on the afternoon of July 20, McDowell issued his battle order for the attack the next morning. His plan was simple but sound. Realizing the center of the Confederate line was too strong for a frontal attack by inexperienced troops, he ordered just a feint there, and then a long flanking march to the right to Sudley and Popular fords to circle and crumple the enemy left. Although McDowell could not know it, the two-day delay in preparing his plan was to prove fatal. Even as he issued his orders the first of Johnston's troops from the valley arrived on the railroad cars at the Junction. When they all got there the Confederates would have about 32,000 men.

Word that the battle would be fought the next day, a Sunday, quickly reached Washington and hundreds of people made frantic preparations to get there to see it. "Every carriage, gig, wagon, and hack has been engaged by people going out to see the fight," wrote an English newspaper reporter. "The French cooks and hotelkeepers, by some occult process of reasoning, have arrived at the conclusion that they must treble the prices of their wines and of the hampers of provisions" the people were ordering to take with them. "Before the battle," wrote a congressman from Ohio, "the hopes of the people and of their representatives are very elated and almost jocosely festive."

The next morning the road to Centreville jammed with nervous horses and handsome carriages, pretty ladies in bright crinoline dresses carrying picnic baskets filled with cool wines and tasty snacks. Senators and congressmen, foreign digni-

fore the battle they knew must come. Yet the camps, like the ones in the North, had a gay, festive atmosphere about them, with constant visitors at all hours of the day and night. In them could be found well-prepared meals, "caddies of tea, barrels of sugar, and many articles better suited for a picnic or a party in a summer house than to soldiers in the field." A young lady visitor wrote that they "were able during those rallying days of June to drive frequently to visit 'the boys' in camp, timing the expeditions to include battalion drill and dress parade, and taking tea afterward in the different tents. Then were the gala days of war, and our proud hosts hastened to produce home dainties dispatched from far-away plantations."

Such was life in the Confederate camps when McDowell left Washington that July 16. Beauregard received word at once that he was coming from a female spy in Washington. Not that it was any secret anyway—everyone in Washington and in the Army knew where they were going. Beauregard immediately requested that Johnston's troops in the valley be sent to him. Two days later the Union Army concentrated on the heights of Centreville overlooking the plains of Manassas as the Confederate outposts fell back to their main line

The first move was to occupy Alexandria, Virginia, just across the Potomac from Washington. Confederate flags flying over the city taunted Lincoln, and on May 24 Colonel Elmer Ellsworth led his Fire Zouaves, now the 11th New York, across the Potomac. (USAMHI)

There Ellsworth saw a Rebel banner flying above the Marshall House. He personally went to the roof and removed it from the staff still visible. On his way to the ground floor, he was met by the house's proprietor, who murdered him on the spot. Ellsworth became the nation's first great martyr, and Lincoln grieved sorely for his dead young friend. (USAMHI)

With Winfield Scott too old to take active field command, a member of his staff, Irvin McDowell, was elevated to brigadier general and given the unenviable task of molding an army and advancing to meet the enemy in Virginia. (USAMHI)

taries, bureaucrats, and reporters, dressed in their light summer clothing and carrying spyglasses and revolvers and flasks of Bourbon, rushed to Virginia to watch the great event, greeting friends, laughing and joking.

To the men in the Union ranks the occasion was not so festive, however. Since two-thirty that morning the flanking march had been taking place under bright moonlight. Across the Turnpike, over Cub Run Creek, through the woods and fields, heading for the Sudley fords. About three hours later, as the first gray streaks of dawn turned the landscape from brown to green, they heard the roar of a Union cannon near the Stone Bridge shatter the early quiet. The first major battle of the

Civil War had begun. By seven o'clock they should have been crossing Bull Run at the fords, but these civilians in uniform could not march that fast. They were still more than two hours away, and already the heat was oppressive. Now they were hot and tired, the fancy uniforms covered with choking dust. Even though the maneuver was already several hours behind schedule, the recruits still straggled after ripe blackberries, stopped for a refreshing drink, or just rested in the shade of the trees. It was about nine-thirty before they reached the fords, and then a Confederate officer high atop a signal tower spotted the glint of the sun on a brass cannon. The surprise was lost.

Quickly the Confederates swung their left flank back to Chinn Ridge behind the Stone House and rushed up reinforcements to counter the threat. Shortly after ten o'clock the Union troops came charging out of the woods into the fields on either side of the Sudley road and drove the Confederates back across the Turnpike to a new position on the plateau around the Henry and Robinson houses. The battle had opened with frightening reality. Yellow sheets of flame flashed along both lines as regiment after regiment exploded into action with a metallic roar. Gigantic crashes of artillery split the air. Shells screamed overhead, exploding in clouds of earth, horses, and men. The noise roared to a crescendo that left men dazed and confused, as the fighting surged back and forth, the issue in doubt, into the afternoon.

On a hill just below Centreville overlooking the plains of Manassas, the carriages from Washington were drawn up as if at a country horse race. Surprisingly, their presence did not seem to bother the troops who saw them. "Near Cub Run we saw carriages and barouches which contained civilians who had driven out from Washington to witness the operation," one soldier remembered. "We thought it wasn't bad idea to have the great men from Washington come out to see us thrash the Rebs." The visitors had a panoramic view of the lovely wooded country, dotted with green fields and cleared lands. According to one observer, "undulating lines of forest marked the course of the streams which intersected it and gave by their variety of color and shading an additional charm to the landscape which, enclosed in a framework of blue and purple hills, softened into violet in the extreme distance, presented one of the most agreeable

*The engineer company of the 8th New York in Arlington, Virginia, in June
1861. Photograph by Brady or an assistant.* (LC)

*Colonel Ambrose Burnside and officers of the 1st Rhode Island Infantry formed
a part of McDowell's developing army.* (USAMHI)

Men of the 1st Rhode Island at Camp Sprague, outside Washington, well trained and ready. (LC)

displays of simple pastoral woodland scenery that could be conceived." Somehow it was difficult to believe that men would actually shoot at and kill each other across this beautiful scene. But then the woods echoed to the roar of cannon, thin lines of dirty gray haze marked the angry muttering of musketry, white puffs of smoke burst high above the treetops, bayonets flashed in the glaring sun, and clouds of dust shifted constantly back and forth across the landscape. One lady spectator with an opera glass "was quite beside herself when an unusually heavy discharge roused the current of her blood—'That is splendid. Oh, my! Is not that first-rate? I guess we will be in Richmond this time tomorrow.'"

All afternoon the battle lines surged back and forth across the plateau, around the Henry House and the Robinson House, on Chinn Ridge, and along the Turnpike as men died by the hundreds in the woods, in the fields, on the banks of Bull Run, in a nightmare battle of mistakes fought by untrained volunteers led by inexperienced officers. Then when the last of Johnston's fresh Confed-

erate troops reached the field late in the afternoon, because the Federal force had failed to hold them in the Shenandoah Valley as planned, McDowell realized any chance of victory was gone and ordered a withdrawal. The exhausted troops started an orderly retreat from the field. The battle was over. "There was no confusion or panic then," one soldier remembered, but the men cursed their generals because they did not have fresh reinforcements as the enemy did. The orderly retreat quickly turned to confusion and then panic when the Confederates pursued, while the civilian spectators and their carriages and buggies created a frenzied jam among the army wagons, caissons, guns, and ambulances. "Infantry soldiers on mules and draft horses with the harness clinging to their heels, as much frightened as their riders," wrote a reporter. "Negro servants on their masters' chargers; ambulances crowded with unwounded soldiers; wagons swarming with men who threw out the contents in the road to make room, grinding through a shouting, screaming mass of men on foot who were literally yelling with rage at every

*The camp of the 1st Minnesota, near Edwards Ferry, Maryland. They were
eager to march south and put down the Rebellion.* (MHS)

*The 2d Michigan came a long way to be in on the one battle that would surely
end the war.* (THE BURTON HISTORICAL COLLECTION, DETROIT PUBLIC LIBRARY)

McDowell marched his arriving regiments across the Long Bridge and others leading from Washington to the Virginia side, and trained and organized his army in and around Arlington. (USAMHI)

He made his headquarters in the stately mansion, Arlington House, that, until a few weeks before, had been the home of Robert E. Lee. Mrs. Lee was still there when he moved in, and he took great care not to discomfort her. Here he planned his campaign. (USAMHI)

halt." No longer under any effective control, many of the soldiers headed for Washington, a confused mob with little semblance of order or discipline. By sundown it was a question of whether or not they should try to make a stand at Centreville. McDowell decided against it. "The condition of our artillery and its ammunition," he reported, "the want of food for the men, and the utter disorganization and demoralization of the mass of the army seemed to admit of no alternative but to fall back."

For miles the roads leading into Washington became strewn with the paraphernalia of war—caps, coats, blankets, rifles, canteens, haversacks. "I saw the beaten, foot-sore, spongy-looking soldiers," a reporter wrote, "officers and all the *debris* of the army filing through mud and rain, forming in crowds in front of the spirit stores." Muddy, hungry, and scared, they staggered through the streets begging food and buying liquor, dropping in exhaustion on porches, lawns, and sidewalks. Many of the younger officers, completely demoralized, filled the hotel barrooms and cheap saloons. One of the civilian casualties who walked forlornly back to Washington was a photographer, already noted for his portraits, who would later become famous, Mathew Brady. He and his assistants had lost the wagon with his camera and all his equipment in the panic, or so he claimed.

And on the plains of Manassas the soul-searing moans of the wounded and dying echoed through the still night air. Motionless forms covered the ground in grotesque positions, as if someone had carelessly heaved them from a wagon. The Federals suffered almost 3,000 casualties in killed, wounded, and missing; the Confederates almost 2,000. All through the night the stretcher-bearers, doctors, friends, and even relatives worked tirelessly among the dead and wounded, the flickering flames from the candles and lanterns casting weird shadows among the dark, silent trees.

"The capture of Washington seems now to be inevitable," a frightened government official declared. "The rout, overthrow, and utter demoralization of the whole army is complete." This, of course, was an exaggeration. A more sober, realistic view of the situation was made by another close observer of the events. "We have undertaken to make war without in the least knowing how," he wrote. "We have made a false start and we have discovered it. It only remains to start afresh." A

Old General Robert Patterson was to keep the Confederate Army of Joseph E. Johnston occupied in the Shenandoah Valley so that it could not reinforce Confederates around Manassas when McDowell attacked them. If Patterson failed, McDowell could be in grave danger. (USAMHI)

lesson had been learned—a hard lesson. It was not going to be a short, easy war. The politicians now realized that all the powerful resources of the North would have to be organized and directed in preparation for a long, bitter struggle. And the war was not going to be won by the theatrical heroics of untrained three-month volunteers and comic opera officers. Large armies would have to be raised, trained, and equipped, with the enlistments for three years or the duration, not three months. Washington would have to be adequately protected against the slightest chance of capture, for if the capital fell there would be no United States as such.

Charles P. Stone, inspector general of the District of Columbia militia, would command one of Patterson's brigades. (USAMHI)

While the North thus learned a vital lesson from this first major defeat, the South seemingly was lulled into a false sense of security by the victory. "We are resting on our oars after the victory at Manassas," a clerk in the War Department in Richmond recorded in his diary. The articulate and observant wife of an aide to President Davis put it more succinctly. "That victory did nothing but send us off into a fool's paradise of conceit, and it roused the manhood of the Northern people." Indeed, there was much indignant criticism of the generals because they did not immediately follow up the victory by marching into Washington right then and there to end the war. But the fact was, as General Johnston tried patiently to explain, that "the Confederate army was more disorganized by victory than that of the United States by defeat." In addition, the men were near exhaustion, they were short on rations and ammunition, the raw troops lacked proper discipline and training, stragglers were numerous, the Federals had erected powerful fortifications around Washington, and the broad Potomac River would have had to be crossed. Also, many of the soldiers now believed the war was just about over anyway. "Exaggerated ideas of the victory among our troops cost us more men than the Federal army lost by defeat," Johnston reported. "Many left the army—not to return." Despite this premature complacency, the South was determined to resist to the bitter end, thus assuring the nation of a long, bloody struggle.

A young lady from Virginia wrote after Manassas:

A few days later we rode over the field. The trampled grass had begun to spring again, and wild flowers were blooming around carelessly made graves. From one of these imperfect mounds of clay I saw a hand extended. . . . Fences were everywhere thrown down; the undergrowth of the woods was riddled with shot; here and there we came upon spiked guns, disabled gun-carriages, cannon balls, blood-stained blankets, and dead horses. We were glad enough to turn away and gallop homeward.

For the men in the armies, however, that homeward turn lay distant years ahead in the uncertain future.

On July 16, 1861, McDowell's army moved out of its camps on the road toward Manassas and the Rebel Army. This image of the 8th New York was taken that same day as they prepared for the march. (MJM)

As they marched they passed historic Falls Church, where George Washington had worshipped. (USAMHI)

They passed by Taylor's Tavern, outside Falls Church, Virginia. (WRHS)

On July 17 the Federals skirmished with the enemy around Fairfax Court House. (WRHS)

And the next day McDowell occupied Centreville, until that morning a fortified Confederate camp. (USAMHI)

From Centreville, McDowell sent Colonel Daniel Tyler forward with his division to reconnoiter the enemy positions along Bull Run. He was ordered not to bring on an engagement. (USAMHI)

Instead Tyler and his chief lieutenant, Colonel Israel B. Richardson, became engaged in a hot fight at Blackburn's Ford, and were repulsed. (PENNSYLVANIA—MOLLUS COLLECTION, WAR LIBRARY AND MUSEUM, PHILADELPHIA)

Three days later, McDowell launched his battle plan, sending his marching columns toward Bull Run, shown here in a July 1862 image by Timothy O'Sullivan. (LC)

Colonel Andrew Porter was next into the fray with his brigade. He felt that Burnside had attacked with "perhaps, too hasty vigor," but he immediately moved to Burnside's support and took command of the division after Hunter's wound. Porter stands at center in this image taken prior to the battle. (P-M)

The 8th New York, perhaps the most resplendent of regiments in McDowell's army, went into battle with Porter. (TERENCE P. O'LEARY)

They were fighting an army led by the hero of Fort Sumter, P. G. T. Beauregard, now a brigadier general in the Confederate Army. (LC)

He made his headquarters behind the lines here at the Wilmer McLean House near McLean's Ford. McLean himself was so disturbed by the war's coming to his very doorstep that he moved where he thought it would never find him again, Appomattox. (WRHS)

Major Samuel Jones was Beauregard's chief of artillery, but, in fact, Confederate cannon would play a minor role in the battle unfolding. (LC)

George Barnard's March 1862 photograph of the battlefield at Bull Run, looking over the Warrenton Turnpike. (USAMHI)

The man who stopped the initial assault by Hunter's column, and several succeeding attacks, thus buying time for Beauregard to rush troops to the threatened left, was another veteran of Fort Sumter. Brigadier General Nathan G. Evans, called "Shanks" by friends, was a rough, uncouth braggart whose orderly always stood behind him with a "barrelita" of whiskey. He would later claim that he alone, with the aid of the Almighty "and a few private gentlemen," won the battle. (SOUTH CAROLINIANA LIBRARY)

A few of those "private gentlemen" who held the line with Evans. Major Roberdeau Wheat's battalion of Louisiana Zouaves, commonly called Wheat's Tigers. They are photographed here in New Orleans in 1861. (LC)

As the battle between Hunter's and Evans's troops developed, Brigadier General Samuel P. Heintzelman's division came into the fight. He, too, would be wounded, but acted heroically in attempting to hold his command together in the confusion of its first fight. (USAMHI)

Soldiers like this rugged-looking woodsman from the 4th Michigan went into the action in Orlando Willcox's brigade of Heintzelman's division. The Michiganders fought like demons, the first Westerners to do battle in the East. (HP)

While the battle raged on the Confederate left,
Colonel William T. Sherman led his brigade
across a ford near the Stone Bridge in the center of
the line and assailed Evans's depleted command.
Sherman is shown here as a major general in an
1865 photo. (NYHS)

Colonel Michael Corcoran, center, and officers of the 69th New York crossed
with Sherman. (MJM)

So did Colonel James Cameron of the 79th New York. The son of Secretary of War Simon Cameron, he would not recross Bull Run. He died in battle. (USAMHI)

Battery E, 3d United States Artillery, commanded by Captain Romeyn B. Ayres. Called Sherman's Battery because it was formerly led by Thomas W. Sherman, this unit was greatly feared by the Confederates because of its mighty Parrot rifles. This image shows the battery on July 24, 1861, in Washington, three days after the battle. (BRUCE GIMELSON)

Erasmus D. Keyes, like Sherman, a colonel of a brigade in Tyler's division, also crossed Bull Run, but played a lesser role in the fighting along the Warrenton Road. (USAMHI)

The 3d Connecticut of Keyes's brigade. Their gallantry, he believed, "was never surpassed." (LC)

The fighting raged first around the Mathews' House on Mathews' Hill, where the advancing Federals slowly forced Evans and his outnumbered command back to the Warrenton Turnpike. (USAMHI)

Evans's command retreated past the Stone House on the Warrenton Road, shown in this March 1862 photo by Barnard and James F. Gibson, and up the slopes of Henry Hill. (USAMHI)

And on Henry Hill the fighting raged for most of the rest of the day. Soon after Evans's arrival, sharp fighting took place on the right of the hill near the Robinson House, where Sherman attacked the line held by yet another veteran of Fort Sumter . . . (USAMHI)

. . . Colonel Wade Hampton, commanding Hampton's Legion. Hampton himself was wounded, but he held his line. (VM)

*Lieutenant Thomas M. Logan of Hampton's
Legion played a conspicuous part in the fighting
around the Robinson House. In February 1865
he would become a brigadier general.* (MC)

*Colonel Francis S. Bartow of Georgia exposed
himself recklessly on the battlefield in leading his
brigade against the Federals. It cost him his life.*
(VM)

The fighting became even more fierce in the center of the Confederate line on Henry Hill. There Brigadier General Barnard E. Bee of South Carolina fought desperately against several enemy assaults. His very presence on the field was a harbinger of victory, for he and his brigade had been sent to Beauregard from the Shenandoah. Johnston had eluded Patterson, and even as the battle raged, more of his regiments were on their way. Bee would fall with a mortal wound, but not before bestowing on another of Johnston's brigade commanders an immortal sobriquet. Attempting to rally his men after a charge, he pointed to a brigade of Virginians behind them and said . . . (VM)

*. . . "There stands Jackson like a stone wall." It was the brigade of Colonel Thomas J. Jackson, shown here in a 1855 daguerreotype. A man of inordinate peculiarities, he would become the greatest legend of the war. (*NATIONAL PORTRAIT GALLERY, SMITHSONIAN INSTITUTION, WASHINGTON, D.C.*)*

Officers of the Washington Artillery of New Orleans, who helped Jackson stand like a wall. They are brothers, Miles Taylor Squires, Samuel Smith Squires, and Charles W. Squires. (W. H. T. SQUIRES, JR.)

The battle raged for hours on Henry Hill, often around the Henry House itself, where poor old widow Henry, who refused to leave, was blown out of her bed by a shell that severed her foot and mortally wounded her. An 1862 view by Durward (USAMHI)

In desperate fighting on the forward slope of
Henry Hill, Captain James B. Ricketts of Battery
I, 1st United States Artillery, was wounded four
times and captured along with all six of his cannon
and forty-nine horses. He would recover to become
a brigadier general in less than a year. (USAMHI)

Nearly as badly used up as Ricketts's battery was
Battery D, 5th United States Artillery. Captain
Charles Griffin obeyed orders to take it nearly to
the brow of the left of Henry Hill. Once there,
Griffin mistook an enemy regiment dressed in blue
for his own troops, and discovered the mistake too
late. All of his cannoneers were shot down and
only three of his six guns escaped, and two of them
had to be abandoned later. (P-M)

Former Governor of Virginia William "Extra
Billy" Smith, now colonel of the 49th Virginia,
took a place in the Confederate line just in time to
assist in the destruction of Ricketts's and Griffin's
batteries. He is shown here in the uniform of a
brigadier general, probably in 1863. (USAMHI)

*Patterson's failure in the Shenandoah allowed Brigadier General Joseph E.
Johnston to bring almost his entire army to assist Beauregard. Johnston arrived
on the field and took overall command of operations the day before the battle.
This rare photo of Johnston has never before been published.* (VM)

Johnston made his headquarters here at the Grigsby House, and directed the movement of brigades and regiments to the battle line, while Beauregard commanded the fighting line in person. (USAMHI)

The unexpected arrival of Johnston's last brigade to reach the field, led by Colonel Arnold Elzey, threw McDowell's right flank into a panic. (VM)

Colonel Oliver O. Howard, commanding a brigade of Heintzelman's division, was at the right flank when Elzey arrived. Heroic efforts by him brought few results, and before he received orders to retire, his men were doing it on their own. He stands at left here, shortly after his promotion to brigadier general. (WRHS)

While his right crumbled into a disorganized retreat, McDowell found his left threatened when Confederates like Colonel Micah Jenkins led the 5th South Carolina across Bull Run. There was little left for McDowell but a general retreat. For Jenkins there would be a brigadier's promotion a year and a day later. (LC)

With the enemy on the run, Brigadier General Milledge L. Bonham's South Carolina brigade took over the pursuit. He would leave the Army in a few months to go to the Confederate Congress, then serve as governor of his state, then don his uniform again in the war's last days. (VM)

Colonel Joseph B. Kershaw spearheaded the pursuit with his 2d South Carolina and, along with old Edmund Ruffin, helped turn retreat into rout when they managed to disable the main bridge over Cub Run that led to safety for the Federals. (SHC)

McDowell's chief of staff, Colonel James B. Fry, made extraordinary efforts to control the retreat, but to no avail. Most of the army did not stop until it reached Centreville, and many soldiers fled all the way to Washington. (P-M)

McDowell had a reserve division commanded by Colonel Dixon S. Miles stationed at Centreville, but Miles took no part in the battle. In fact, he got drunk and could not give coherent orders to his officers. (USAMHI)

Miles's soldiers, like flamboyant Colonel Louis Blenker, shown here with men of the 8th New York, chafed at being left out of the battle. Standing just left of Blenker is Lieutenant Colonel Julius Stahel. In two weeks Blenker will be a brigadier . . . (NA)

. . . and Stahel will get his first star in November. These German and Hungarian officers were enormously popular, and the Lincoln Administration hoped that giving them high command would encourage the thousands of their nationality in the North to enlist. It also put great responsibility in the hands of men with little ability. (USAMHI)

Another popular foreigner, Colonel Frederick G. D'Utassy (third from the right) and the staff of his 39th New York, the "Garibaldi Guard." They, too, sat out the battle at Centreville. (MJM)

And for some who missed the fight, the war was already over. The 4th New Jersey and its officers shown here mustered out of service ten days after the battle. (USAMHI)

*Still, there were many heroes of the battle. One was the son of amateur
photographer—and now quartermaster general of the Union
Army—Montgomery C. Meigs. John R. Meigs served as a volunteer aide to
Colonel Israel Richardson. "A braver and more gallant young man was never
in any service," said Richardson. Here his father photographed him and his
sister on his return from the battle, perhaps looking at the elder Meigs's own
stereo photographs. Three years later, in the Shenandoah, Confederate
guerrillas would kill him.* (LC)

The famous "Sherman Battery" came through the battle with all of its guns, and was the object of much curiosity afterward. Here, again, it was photographed in Washington. (MHS)

For many of the Bull Run regiments, defeat or not, there was a triumphal welcome when they returned home to muster out of service. Many of these were three- and nine-month regiments. They will be replaced by regiments enlisted for three years or the war. The North now knew that it would not be over quickly. The return of the 1st Michigan for mustering out in Detroit, August 7, 1861. (BURTON HISTORICAL COLLECTION, DETROIT PUBLIC LIBRARY)

For many of the men of Bull Run, however, there was no welcome home.
Hundreds were captured and sent south to makeshift prisons. Many, like these
men of Corcoran's 69th New York, were placed in Castle Pinckney at
Charleston. They kept their spirits high, lightheartedly decorating their quarters
with a sign reading "Music Hall 444 Broadway." (USAMHI)

Men of Cameron's 79th New York suffer the same fate. (VM)

And Irvin McDowell will not go unscathed. Not entirely to blame for his loss, still he must be replaced. A new general from the west comes to take over, a man with Napoleonic pretensions and the nickname "Little Mac," Major General George B. McClellan. For the next year the war in the East will be his war. He stands at center here, hand in blouse, with the principal generals of the Army in August 1861. From the left they are Brigadier General William F. Smith, Brigadier General William B. Franklin, Heintzelman, Porter, McDowell, McClellan, Major General George McCall, Brigadier General Don Carlos Buell, Blenker, Brigadier General Silas Casey, and Brigadier General Fitz John Porter. They pose with hats on . . . (LC)

. . . and with hats off. (AMERICANA IMAGE GALLERY)

But many will never pose again. Barnard's 1862 photograph of the rude graves of Federal soldiers buried by the Confederates at Bull Run. (KA)

Barnard's 1862 image of a "hecatomb" where 100 Union soldiers sleep below the Sudley Church. For them the war was over. (KA)

The Navies Begin

VIRGIL CARRINGTON JONES

Improvisation and innovative technology clash on the water

EVEN BEFORE the Confederate triumph at Bull Run, the Civil War enhanced the stature of Stephen Russell Mallory, Confederate Secretary of the Navy. He took office and accepted the seemingly impossible task of sending against the enemy a fleet that did not exist. At the end of 1861, however, he had things so well organized that he was posing a threat which caused the Union to try to find effective ways to stop him.

Little about Mallory as an individual explained why the President of the new-born Confederate States of America, Jefferson Davis, so quickly singled him out for the job he held. He was rather naive and had dabbled at various occupations—town marshal, real estate dealer, admiralty lawyer, county judge, customs collector, newspaper correspondent, political leader. At age twenty-four he had had a touch of soldiery in the Seminole War. And then, in 1851, he was elected to the United States Senate from Florida, serving in that capacity for ten years and rising in time to the chairmanship of the important Naval Affairs Committee, a responsibility that unquestionably drew Davis's attention to him.

As his record shows, he was in no sense a quitter. This was demonstrated in his wooing of a Spanish beauty who was bored by his manners at first, but later accepted his proposal of marriage. It was a trait that stood him in good stead when the burden of creating a navy was placed upon his shoulders. While participating in a losing cause, he strove so diligently to succeed that he helped revolutionize the field of naval science. Under his guidance, the Confederacy took part in history's first battle between ironclads, produced the first submarine to sink a ship, and developed the underwater mine or torpedo as an effective weapon of defense.

The war still was nearly two months away when Mallory took office, but the threat was strong. Ominously, the widely scattered ships of the Union began sailing homeward, some of them steering for southern ports. At the mouth of the Mississippi River, vessels passing up or downstream were searched. Floridians surprised and captured the United States Coast Survey schooner *Dana*.

Some of the seceded states demanded that Union ships within their ports be turned over to them. Among the commanders who refused to do so and fled with their vessels were John Newland Maffitt, later an outstanding Confederate naval officer, and David D. Porter, equally as staunch a Unionist.

Leaders who formed the nucleus of the Confederacy gathered in early February at Montgomery,

The U.S.S. Constitution, *symbol of past naval glory, and of an out-of-date
United States fleet in 1861.* (LC)

Alabama. Even before the government was organized, a committee was named to summon "all such persons versed in naval affairs as they may deem advisable to consult with." Only a few United States Navy officers of high rank—five captains and four commanders—had "gone South" at this time, their action hinging on the secession of their respective states. Nevertheless, telegrams were immediately sent to all officers thought to be southern in their sympathy. The response was favorable. By June, a fifth of the officers so contacted had resigned, among them sixteen captains, thirty-four commanders, and seventy-six lieutenants.

One of these officers was Commander Raphael Semmes, a member of the Lighthouse Board at Washington and only a short period away from one of the most outstanding privateering careers in history. Another was John M. Brooke, already recognized for the banded guns of his own design he was having manufactured at the Tredegar Iron Works in Richmond. Still another was John Taylor Wood, Naval Academy instructor and grandson of President Zachary Taylor.

When the Confederate Navy was created by formal act, it was soon announced that it was to be headed by chubby-faced, side-whiskered Mallory. He took office immediately, heading a fleet that existed only on paper. He had little to draw from. The South possessed virtually no merchant bottoms, no large force of skilled mechanics, and only a few seamen, for seafaring pursuits were not a favorite among its people. It had only two navy yards, one at Pensacola, Florida, and one at Norfolk, Virginia; only three rolling mills, two in Tennessee and one in Georgia, the latter unfitted for heavy work; and no machine shops of superior workmanship. Its sole foundry capable of casting heavy guns was at Richmond, soon to replace Montgomery as the capital of the Confederacy. The only raw material available was standing timber. All else, including iron, would have to be acquired. Only seven steam war vessels had ever been built in the South, and the engines of only two of these had been contracted for in the states involved.

Confronting Mallory as Union Secretary of the Navy was Gideon Welles, described as a small-town politician. His task would be one of organization, for the fleet at his disposal was recognized as third in world power. It consisted of eighty-nine vessels, forty-two in commission, twenty-six available but not in commission, and twenty-one rated unserviceable. Although considered very slow, Welles took immediate action for the purchase of 136 vessels, to be altered and commissioned, and the construction of fifty-two others.

Abraham Lincoln's inauguration on March 4 added to the burden Mallory faced, for the new President announced a policy of reoccupying and holding the forts in the South. As the approach to the most important of these was by water, it meant the Confederacy must do something promptly about its deficiency in naval armament. Water mines were settled upon as the answer.

Along with the South's plans for a navy also came the original move for the training of personnel. At Montgomery on March 16, the Congress passed an act providing for a Confederate States Naval Academy, but it would be 1863 before steps actually were taken to bring such a facility into service. At this later period, an academy was actually set up in Richmond and the steamer *Patrick Henry,* formerly of the James River squadron, was used as a schoolship. The Union in the meantime took action to protect its important Naval Academy at Annapolis, Maryland. Because of its proximity to southern soil, it was transferred, along with its training ship, to Newport, Rhode Island.

On April 1, Commander Semmes, who had been sent North on a buying tour, detrained at Montgomery. He had had little success, finding no ships available which were suitable for service on the high seas. The only purchase he had made was a large amount of ordnance stores. Meanwhile, James D. Bullock, captain of the United States mail steamer *Bienville,* and another who had resigned to side with the South were dispatched to England to make arrangements for the construction of ships.

The fall of Fort Sumter was simultaneous with one of Lincoln's most important decisions, for on this same date, April 14, 1861, the sailing frigate *Sabine,* equipped with forty-four guns, began a blockade at Pensacola. Soon it would be extended along the entire southern coast—more than 3,500 miles, the longest ever attempted by any nation—and eventually would rank as one of the North's most effective steps of offense.

Two days later, Lincoln issued a call for 75,000 troops. A counter proclamation came from Presi-

*The Navy Department in Washington, faced with the herculean task of
building quickly a new navy to blockade the southern coast and conquer its
rivers. To organize and run this mammoth undertaking, Lincoln selected . . .*
(LC)

dent Davis on April 17, an offer of letters of
marque under the seal of the Confederate States
against ships and property of the United States.
This was a direct strike against the Union's extensive merchant fleet.

The seventeenth brought other important action.
Virginia seceded, affording an answer as to what
was to be done with the Gosport Navy Yard at
Norfolk, one of the largest in the nation. For
weeks, the North had been undecided, withholding
action in the hope that Virginia would remain in
the Union. When the state seceded, officials at
Washington decided to abandon the yard. This
was one of the greatest strokes of luck that Mallory
would have in his efforts to build a navy.

While ships and buildings at the yard were set
afire before they were abandoned, Southerners
moved in time to salvage much of what was at
hand. Six ships, among them the *Merrimack*, the
drydock, large supplies of ammunition and food,
and more than a thousand guns were recovered.
Without these guns, the Confederacy would have
had to wait for months to arm some of its posts.
And on April 18, the *Sumter*, a passenger ship con-

verted into a raider, slipped out of the port of New
Orleans. At its helm was Raphael Semmes, com-
mencing the career that would afford him his place
in history. Before the end of the war, he would
capture 305 ships, bond ten of them and burn
fifty-five, making a contribution in money and destruction valued at more than $5,000,000.

By May, the South had the nucleus of a navy—
ten vessels carrying fifteen guns. Some had been
seized, some purchased, and some were captured
slavers. The Confederacy was not alone in its quest
for additional craft. The United States was just
as persistent and soon acquired every available
steamer in Canada.

Mallory became more and more convinced that
ironclad ships would help substantially in offsetting
the South's fleet discrepancy. On May 8, he wrote:
"I regard the possession of an iron-armored ship as
a matter of the first necessity. Such a vessel at this
time could traverse the entire coast of the United
States, prevent all blockades, and encounter, with a
fair prospect of success, their entire navy."

His reference to the blockade was at the moment
no exaggeration. All along the Atlantic coast it

. . . a Connecticut newspaperman, Gideon Welles. He wore an ill-fitting wig, lacked humor, and proved to be one of the most capable and loyal members of Lincoln's Cabinet. (NA)

was mostly a matter of bluff. Lincoln realized this and appointed an overall commander to strengthen it. The assignment went to Commodore Silas H. Stringham, a born seaman and experienced officer. Almost at the same time, the North took steps to block the Mississippi River. They were encouraged by James B. Eads, a veteran shipbuilder thoroughly familiar with the western rivers, who came to Washington to propose blocking the Mississippi to commerce, thereby shutting off a main artery by which the Confederacy could get food, as well as an important route by which it could move cotton to sea. Commander John Rodgers, capable and

efficient, was assigned the task of developing a naval force along that major stream.

By July, Mallory was able to report:

The frigate *Merrimack* has been raised and docked at an expense of $6,000, and the necessary repairs to hull and machinery to place her in her former condition is estimated by experts at $450,000. The vessel would then be in the river, and by the blockade of the enemy's fleets and batteries rendered comparatively useless. It has, therefore, been determined to shield her completely with three-inch iron, placed at such angles as to render her ball-proof, to complete her at the earliest moment, to arm her with the heaviest ordnance, and to send her at once against the enemy's fleet. It is believed that thus prepared she will be able to contend successfully against the heaviest of the enemy's ships, and to drive them from Hampton Roads and the ports of Virginia.

The *Merrimack* was only one phase of the Confederacy's program to provide its navy with ironclad ships. As it was considered impracticable to purchase these in Europe, plans were pursued to build them in the waters of the South. Contracts were let for a supply of all classes of iron. In this connection, it was learned that the Union was preparing an ironclad fleet of gunboats at St. Louis, Missouri. The Navy Department at Richmond sent reliable mechanics to that city to obtain employment on the vessels and to report on their strength and fighting character, as well as the progress made on them. In time, this information was made available to Mallory, influencing him to concentrate on the defense of New Orleans against an attack from above rather than from the Gulf of Mexico.

The first attack would come elsewhere, however. By August, the North was ready to launch a naval blow against the South. So far as the blockade was concerned, the seat of troubles was at Hatteras on the North Carolina coast. Since May, it had developed into a haven for both runners and privateers, creating such a threat to northern commerce that newspapers referred to it as "a nest for pirates." Hampered by a succession of gales, a fleet for an expedition against Hatteras slowly assembled in

He found on taking office a fleet that was old and wooden. The U.S.S. Ohio
was an obsolete ship of the line built more than forty years before. (USAMHI)

War of 1812 frigates like the Santee *and* Constitution *were still in service and
totally unsuited for the war to come. They are shown here at Annapolis,
Maryland, at the United States Naval Academy.* (USAMHI)

Many of the personnel were even older and more out of date. Captain William B. Shubrick had been in the Navy since 1806 and served aboard the Constitution *in the War of 1812.* (USAMHI)

Hampton Roads under the direction of Major General John E. Wool, commanding at Fort Monroe. Foremost among the vessels it consisted of were the flagship *Minnesota,* the *Wabash, Cumberland, Monticello, Pawnee,* and *Harriet Lane,* as well as three troop carriers, the steamers *Adelaide* and *George Peabody,* and the tug *Fanny.* The frigate *Susquehanna* would join it at its destination. On August 26, the ships started moving southward. At four o'clock the next afternoon, they were sighted off Hatteras.

Early on the morning of the twenty-eighth, the signal for a landing was given. The South had nothing on hand with which to combat such a fleet, and Forts Clark and Hatteras, defending the point, lowered their flags within a matter of hours. The surrender gave the North a foothold along the southern coast and put it in possession of the main passage to the North Carolina sounds. It was the first sizable victory for the Union since its troops

had suffered defeat in the Battle of Bull Run. Prisoners included 670 officers and men. Guns found in the forts had been a part of the armament made available to the Confederates on the abandonment of the Gosport Navy Yard.

The moral effect of the victory was most important, for there were indications that the South was moving ahead in its efforts to build a navy, as well as to arm its troops. The United States consul at London reported the Rebel agents, with more funds at their control than previously, were buying at random. He revealed that the ship *Bermuda* had sailed from England with a million-dollar cargo made up of cannon, rifles, powder, cartridges, and other munitions of war. Her destination was Savannah, Georgia.

Also, the South's shipbuilding program had been stepped up considerably. Construction of two warships, the *Arkansas* and the *Tennessee,* had been started at Memphis, while two others, the *Missis-*

Flag Officer Charles Stewart, senior officer in the Navy, had been born in 1778, and commanded the Constitution *when Shubrick served aboard her. He was eighty-three years old when war broke out and still on the active list.* (NYHS)

sippi and the *Louisiana,* were under way at New Orleans. Lieutenant Bullock, meanwhile, was meeting with success in England. He had arranged for the building of two vessels, the *Florida* and the *Alabama,* that would eventually become grave threats to the North's ocean-going commerce. In addition, individual states were forming their own navies, later to be turned over to the Confederacy. South Carolina in March had prepared for sea the first ship she had launched since the Revolution.

As Mallory hurriedly pressed forward, October found the North ready for its second naval expedition. This time the destination was Port Royal Sound, a body of water on the coast of South Carolina. Early in the war, the Union Navy Department listed it as one of three points that would serve as bases from which to combat blockade running. So easily could it be defended that the Federals feared the Confederates would make it impregnable before it could be taken over.

Again the starting point was Hampton Roads. There, under the command of Commodore Samuel Francis du Pont, head of Lincoln's Naval Advisory Board, a fleet of fifty ships assembled. The expedition sailed on October 29 amid much secrecy. But within a matter of hours after the fleet started moving, the Confederacy's Acting Secretary of War, Judah P. Benjamin, was able to wire military authorities at Savannah that the destination was Port Royal. This warning did little good. The Confederates again had nothing to stop a powerful fleet. The forts at Port Royal quickly fell.

While the North now had two naval victories to its credit, it still aimed no decisive blow at the South. By November, the blockade runners were nearing the peak of their activity. Eight out of every nine were getting into port, picking their destinations at random and using every trick to avoid the blockaders. It was not long before lanterns went out of style among the Union vessels standing guard off the southern coast, for it was found these lights at night were like buoys to the ships trying to

make shore. Meanwhile Mallory, by December, had a fleet he no longer could count on his fingers. Thirty-five ships and sailing craft of various classes and armaments had been equipped by the Confederacy. Twenty-one of these were steam vessels, most of them small and built for speed rather than power. A majority had fewer than five guns. Some were protected by bales of cotton. He had entered into thirty-two contracts for the construction of forty gunboats, floating batteries, and vessels of war. In addition, the Navy Department had vessels under construction at its own direction. Progress was made in other quarters. A powder mill, engine mill, boiler mill, machine shops, and ordnance workshops were erected. Also completed was a ropewalk capable of making all kinds of cordage, from a rope yard to a nine-inch cable, with a capacity of 8,000 yards a month.

At Washington, Navy Secretary Welles also had been busy. By December, the Union fleet consisted of 264 vessels, carrying 2,557 guns and manned by 22,000 seamen. But the imbalance between the two navies was not the point of interest at this stage of the war. Rather, attention focused on the blockade runners. They brought the guns and ammunition, the vital items needed to make the Confederacy's armies more formidable, more able to repeat their early victories. The runners would have to continue to bear this responsibility until the South could further expand its facilities. Mallory had started office with appropriations of only $17,300. In the first eighteen months of operations, he would have available $14,605,777.

In the offing, he gained a reputation of doing much with nothing. But time would bring a kaleidoscopic pattern as the Union armies marched southward and the Union fleets gave them much-needed support in times of desperation. And after the initial Union successes at Hatteras and Port Royal, the focus of attention, land and water, turned to the West.

But there was new blood, and wood, in the Navy as well. The U.S.S. Hartford was a powerful 24-gun sloop launched in 1858, shown here after her commissioning at the Boston Navy Yard in 1859. (LC)

And promising younger officers like David D. Porter, son of an earlier naval hero and brother of "Dirty Bill" Porter, who would serve on the Mississippi. (USAMHI)

As in all navies in all times, Welles would find more than enough eager young officers hoping to see action after he retired the men now too old to command. (NAVAL HISTORICAL CENTER)

Sailors must be enlisted to crew the growing fleet. A naval recruiting station at the Battery in New York City. They advertised a bounty of $400 to those who would enlist. (WENDELL W. LANG, JR.)

Time did not allow the building of a complete fleet. To have a Union naval presence in the South's waters as soon as possible, Welles bought merchant steamers and even New York ferry boats like the Commodore Perry *and converted them quickly into river gunboats.* (USAMHI)

There was also the safety of the Naval Academy to consider. At Annapolis it was too exposed and vulnerable to Confederate sympathizers in Maryland. (USAMHI)

Welles moved it temporarily to Newport, Rhode Island, where it continued to produce officers for the Union, as this class in 1863. (NHC)

And this group of stern-faced young Nelsons. (RP)

The midshipman of 1861 could affect a jaunty air, but many felt grave fears that there would not be enough action for them in this war. (USAMHI)

They learned the art of naval gunnery . . . (NA)

The officers of the Bureau of Steam Engineering, and seated at center, Chief Engineer Benjamin F. Isherwood. They supervised the Union's construction program for steam war vessels. They designed and built the engines that drove the Federal Navy. (USAMHI)

September 17, 1864, the launch of the frigate U.S.S. Franklin *at the Portsmouth, New Hampshire, Navy Yard—a common scene in the years after Welles took command. This screw frigate itself never saw action.* (NA)

Then came the time for offensive action. Commodore Silas H. Stringham, one of Welles's most trusted confidants, commanded the Atlantic blockading squadron and planned and led the successful attack on Fort Hatteras. (USAMHI)

Captain Samuel Barron, the unsuccessful Confederate defender at Hatteras, spent eleven months in prison after his capture. (CHS)

The steam frigate Minnesota, *Stringham's flagship in the attack on Forts Clark and Hatteras.* (NA)

Port Royal, South Carolina, the next scene of Union naval victory. A Timothy O'Sullivan photograph, probably taken in early 1862. (USAMHI)

The U.S.S. Wabash, *flagship of Captain Samuel F. I. du Pont, standing in the center of the group of three officers. In it he led the attack on Port Royal.* (USAMHI)

Captain Charles H. Davis, fleet captain of Du Pont's seventeen ships as they attacked Forts Walker and Beauregard. (USAMHI)

The deck of the U.S.S. Pawnee, *an early veteran of the attempt to relieve Sumter, and the attacks on Hatteras Inlet and Port Royal. The screw sloop will be part of the backbone of the blockade in the years to come.* (CHS)

O'Sullivan's photograph of the Coosaw Ferry to Port Royal Island. (USAMHI)

A Federal pontoon wharf at Coosaw Ferry after the capture of Port Royal. (NYHS)

Confederate Fort Walker on Hilton Head, seen from the rear, by O'Sullivan.
(USAMHI)

Fort Beauregard, showing ten heavy guns within its earthworks. From its commanding position on Bay Point, it still could not deter Du Pont's fleet. (USAMHI)

The interior of Fort Beauregard, the Union's first strong foothold in South Carolina. (USAMHI)

O'Sullivan's 1862 photograph of one of the Confederate guns inside Fort Beauregard. (USAMHI)

The Mills Plantation on Port Royal Island, where life went on much as usual. (USAMHI)

Members of the 79th New York, veterans of Bull Run, could be happy about a victory for a change. After the battle they built this mock battery at Seabrooke Point on Port Royal Island. (USAMHI)

Quickly the Union took advantage of its capture, and enhanced it. The wharf at Hilton Head that fed a constant stream of supplies to the South Carolina Federals. (USAMHI)

A man torn by conflicting loyalties. Commander Percival Drayton was a native of South Carolina, yet he stayed with the Union. He commanded the U.S.S. Pocahontas in the attack on Hilton Head. The commander of the Confederates defending Hilton Head was . . . (USAMHI)

. . . his brother, Brigadier General Thomas F. Drayton. (USAMHI)

*The boat landing at Beaufort began to
bustle with Federal craft.* (USAMHI)

*Private homes like the Fuller House
became officers' headquarters.* (USAMHI)

The generals, like Isaac I. Stevens seated here for O'Sullivan, were a commonplace sight. (SOUTH CAROLINA HISTORICAL SOCIETY)

And the price of any great gain in this war, the graves of the dead. Eight men were killed aboard Du Pont's ships. They are buried here on Hilton Head. Photograph by O'Sullivan. (USAMHI)

*By November 16, 1861, with two significant successes to its credit, the Union
Navy could justifiably preen for its President. The men of the U.S.S. Pensacola
man the yards in honor of a visit in Alexandria by Abraham Lincoln.* (WRHS)

With war coming to the West, troops must be raised. Existing units, like the Kentucky State Guard, provided many companies already trained and equipped for the Confederacy. Standing at center, in the top hat, is Kentucky's governor, Beriah Magoffin, in this August 1860 photograph. When called on to furnish volunteers to suppress the Rebellion, he refused to aid "the wicked purpose" with Kentucky soldiers. (KHS)

on February 14. The following day the Confederates almost broke out to the south—indeed, probably would have had not their commander, Brigadier General John Floyd, lost his nerve. On the other hand, Grant, again applying the lesson he had learned in Missouri, promptly counterattacked and drove the Rebels back into their fortifications.

On February 16 Brigadier General Simon Bolivar Buckner, who had succeeded Floyd as commander, asked Grant for terms. Grant replied: "No terms except unconditional and immediate surrender. . . . I propose to move immediately upon your works." Buckner had no choice except

to comply. Close to 12,000 Confederates became prisoners of war.

It was the biggest Union victory so far in the war. Along with the fall of Fort Henry it opened middle Tennessee to Federal invasion via the Cumberland and Tennessee rivers, made Polk's position at Columbus untenable, and forced Johnston to retreat hastily from Kentucky all the way to Corinth, Mississippi.

There he began concentrating his hitherto scattered forces. By April he had 40,000 troops organized into four divisions commanded by generals Polk, Braxton Bragg, William J. Hardee, and

John C. Breckinridge. On April 3 he set out to attack Grant at Pittsburg Landing on the Tennessee. His plan, which had been devised by General P. G. T. Beauregard, who had been posted from Virginia to serve as second-in-command in the West, was to surprise and destroy Grant's 42,000-man army before it was joined by another large Union force under Major General Don Carlos Buell heading down from Nashville. If successful, central Tennessee would be redeemed and the tide of the war in the West reversed.

It was only twenty miles from Corinth to Pittsburg Landing. But the roads were bad and the march discipline of the raw Rebel troops worse. Hence, instead of striking Grant on the morning of April 5 as planned, the Confederates found themselves on the evening of that day still several miles from their objective. Beauregard, despairing of achieving surprise, advised returning to Corinth. However, Johnston, believing that a retreat would

be more demoralizing than a defeat, ordered the attack to be made at dawn on April 6.

And so it was—and with great success. Despite the fact that some of their patrols had heard, seen, and even clashed with advance units of Johnston's army, most of the Federals were taken by surprise. Grant, who had been promoted to major general for Fort Donelson, simply had not expected Johnston to bring the battle to him. Furthermore, he had posted his troops with a view to drilling rather than defense—nor, as usual during the early period of the war, had they bothered to entrench. Consequently the Confederates, charging with a ferocity that henceforth would be their trademark, drove back Grant's men, thousands of whom fled in wild-eyed panic. It seemed that Johnston's prediction to his staff as the battle got under way, "Tonight we will water our horses in the Tennessee River," would come true.

However, most of the Northerners fought with a

Officers of the Kentucky State Guard at Louisville in August 1860. Almost all of them will become Confederates. The officer at right shaking hands with a civilian is Colonel Thomas H. Hunt, who would later command the 9th Kentucky Infantry in the celebrated Orphan Brigade. (KHS)

stubbornness equal to the Southerners' dash. In particular several thousand of them under Brigadier General Benjamin Prentiss, stationed in a sunken road which soon and ever after was called The Hornets' Nest, repulsed assault after assault. Nearby, scores of wounded from both sides mingled as they sought to quench their thirst in "The Bloody Pond." At 2:30 P.M., Johnston, while urging his men on against the Yankee strongpoint, bled to death when a bullet severed an artery in his right leg. Not until late in the afternoon, after surrounding him, did the Confederates force Prentiss to surrender. By then Grant had been able to form a compact defense line around Pittsburg Landing with his 7,000 remaining effectives, who were bolstered by massed artillery, gunboats, and several regiments from the vanguard of Buell's army. When at twilight a few thousand exhausted Rebels —the most Beauregard, who had replaced Johnston, could muster—made a last desperate effort to drive the Federals into the river, withering fire flung them back.

It was a hideous night of torrential rain falling on thousands of untended, moaning, screaming wounded. During the night 5,000 Union troops under Brigadier General Lew Wallace, who had been encamped to the north of Pittsburg Landing, belatedly joined Grant's army. More importantly, 20,000 of Buell's men also arrived. In the morning Grant counterattacked. Beauregard, who had no more than 20,000 muskets in his firing line, slowly gave way. Finally, late in the afternoon, seeing that victory was impossible and defeat inevitable, he ordered a retreat back to Corinth. The Federals, happy to see the Confederates leave, did not pursue.

Pittsburg Landing, as the North called it, or Shiloh, as the South named it after a log church around which much of the fighting centered, was the biggest and bloodiest battle of the war to that time. Nearly 11,000 Confederates and over 13,000 Federals were killed, wounded, captured, or missing—a loss for each army of 25 per cent of the troops actually engaged. Strategically it clinched

The Federals flocked to the banners in even greater numbers; here a group of Iowa volunteers pose in their training camp. (MISSOURI HISTORICAL SOCIETY)

Officers of the 1st Minnesota gather at the home of the commandant at Fort Snelling in May 1861, ready to go to war. (MHS)

the Union gains resulting from Forts Henry and Donelson. Psychologically it was a tremendous blow to Confederate morale and gave the northern soldiers of the West something of the same sense of superiority that the Southerners in Virginia derived from Bull Run. Yet if Johnston had been able to attack on the day planned, probably he would have destroyed Grant, although it is unlikely that his army would have been in condition to follow up the victory.

As it was, the Federals failed to exploit fully their success. After the battle Major General Henry W. Halleck, overall Union commander in the West, took personal charge of operations. He soon revealed himself to be more at home at a desk than in the saddle. Although he accumulated over 120,000 men, he moved with excessive slowness and caution on Corinth, where Beauregard, despite reinforcements from the Trans-Mississippi under Major Generals Earl Van Dorn and Sterling Price, mustered barely 50,000. Then, when he finally forced Beauregard to evacuate Corinth on June 7, he neither pursued nor struck for Vicksburg, which

as a result of the Union captures of Island No. 10, Fort Pillow, and Memphis during the spring was the last remaining major Confederate stronghold on the Mississippi north of Baton Rouge. Instead he broke up his host into a number of separate armies spread between Memphis and the approaches to Chattanooga. By so doing he gave the Confederates, now commanded by Bragg, a breathing spell which they put to good use.

Kentucky and Tennessee were not the only western states to witness a Confederate rollback during the early months of 1862. The same occurred from the opposite direction in Louisiana and Mississippi. On the night of April 24, in a daring surprise move, Flag Officer David Farragut, United States Navy, ran his wooden warships past Forts St. Philip and Jackson guarding the mouth of the Mississippi. A Confederate attempt to stop him with gunboats, rams, and fire rafts failed, and on the afternoon of April 25 he seized New Orleans, the South's largest city and main port. He then proceeded up the river to capture Baton Rouge on May 12 and Natchez six days later.

"We are coming, Father Abraham," they sang. The 28th Wisconsin, bound for Kentucky. (NA)

However, strong fortifications and the powerful ironclad *Arkansas* foiled him at Vicksburg during June and July.

Meanwhile, Union troops commanded by Ben Butler, a political general from Massachusetts, garrisoned New Orleans. There some of the women expressed their resentment of the Yankee presence by spitting on blue-clad soldiers. In retaliation Butler on May 15 issued an order declaring that "hereafter when any female shall by word, gesture, or movement insult . . . any officer or soldier of the United States she shall be regarded and held liable to be treated as woman of the town plying her vocation." This order enraged Southerners, who denounced Butler as a "beast." But it stopped the spitting.

Numerous male Louisianans expressed their opposition to northern rule by forming guerrilla bands which harassed Federal outposts and shipping. On May 28 forty of these bushwhackers fired on a boat from Farragut's flagship *Hartford,* which was putting ashore at Baton Rouge. Outraged, Farragut promptly opened up with his heavy cannons, wrecking the state capitol along with many other buildings.

Not all Louisianans resisted Yankee domination.

Hundreds of free blacks—many of whom were in fact white-skinned—joined the 1st Louisiana Native Guards, the formation of which had been authorized by Butler on August 22, a full month before Lincoln issued the Preliminary Emancipation Proclamation. Mustered in at New Orleans on September 27, it was one of the first Negro regiments to serve in the Union Army.

Baton Rouge suffered further devastation on August 5 when 2,600 Confederates under Breckinridge tried to retake it. At first they drove the 2,500-man Union garrison toward the river. But then they came under heavy fire from gunboats and eventually retreated. Plans had called for the ironclad *Arkansas* to assist Breckinridge's assault, but owing to engine trouble she failed to arrive in time and on the following day her crew blew her up in order to prevent her capture by Federal warships. Both sides lost heavily at Baton Rouge, with the northern commander, Brigadier General Thomas Williams, being among the slain.

Six days after the battle the Federals evacuated the town, which was given over to pillaging and burning by Negroes and convicts released from the state prison. As for Breckinridge, he withdrew to Port Hudson, where he fortified the bluff overlook-

The status of Kentucky, key to Union and Confederate war plans, was precarious. Declared neutral, she had to depend on both sides to honor that stance. Neither did. Major General George B. McClellan, commanding Ohio state forces in April and May, refused to recognize that neutrality, and thereby helped hold Kentucky in the Union. An 1861 photograph by the Brady studio. (USAMHI)

ing the Mississippi. The approximately 150-mile-stretch between that point and Vicksburg constituted the last link between the eastern and western halves of the Confederacy.

In northern Mississippi Bragg spent the early part of the summer reorganizing and training the army he had taken over from Beauregard. His men hated his harsh discipline and him for it, but they became better soldiers and, perhaps, even better fighters. By late July he was ready to launch an offensive which had as its object nothing less than the liberation of Tennessee and the occupation of Kentucky. Leaving behind 15,000 men under Sterling Price to keep an eye on Grant in West Tennes-

see and another small army under Van Dorn to guard Vicksburg, he transferred his remaining 35,000 troops by rail from Tupelo through Mobile and Atlanta to Chattanooga. By this maneuver, the most brilliant of its kind during the war, he outflanked the entire Federal front in the West. In addition, raids by the hard-riding gray troopers of Frank Armstrong, Nathan Bedford Forrest, and John Hunt Morgan caused Buell's army, which had been slowly advancing on Chattanooga, to fall back to Nashville, thus opening a path into Kentucky.

On August 28 Bragg began marching north. "Fighting Joe" Wheeler's cavalry led the way; the infantry jubilantly sang "Dixie." Two days later another Confederate army, 7,000 men under Major General Edmund Kirby Smith, who had moved up from Knoxville, routed 6,500 Federals at Richmond, Kentucky, then occupied Lexington. Expecting to be attacked next, the people of Cincinnati frantically constructed fortifications as thousands of Ohio and Kentucky militia hastened to their aid. But Kirby Smith neither advanced northward against Cincinnati nor moved westward to reinforce Bragg: He was too cautious to do the former and too reluctant to give up his quasi-independent command to do the latter.

All the while Buell, believing that Bragg was aiming for Nashville, remained at the Tennessee capital with his 50,000 troops. Not until September 7 did he realize that the Confederate objective was Kentucky and so set out in pursuit.

Given his long lead, Bragg by rapid marching might have taken Louisville—a stroke which would have panicked the Northwest. However, Davis had instructed him not to take unnecessary risks, and he feared being caught between the forces protecting that city and Buell's army moving up from Tennessee. Therefore, after capturing a 4,000-man Federal garrison at Munfordville, Kentucky, on September 17, 1862 (the same day as the Battle of Antietam), he swerved eastward to link up with Kirby Smith. Ten days later Buell reached Louisville, where he began readying a counteroffensive. His preparations were somewhat disrupted when on September 29 Brigadier General Jefferson C. Davis murdered Brigadier General William "Bull" Nelson after the three-hundred-pound Nelson slapped him during an altercation at a hotel.

Back to the south: Price, having been instructed

By the fall, Federal recruiting and training camps appeared in the Bluegrass, at places like Camp Nelson, complete with bakeries . . . (NA, U. S. WAR DEPT. GENERAL STAFF)

. . . well-supplied workshops . . . (NA, U. S. SIGNAL CORPS)

. . . and even reservoirs with picket fences. (NA, U. S. SIGNAL CORPS)

by Bragg to enter middle Tennessee, advanced to Iuka, in northeastern Mississippi, on September 14. Grant countered by sending a column under Major General William S. Rosecrans to strike Price from the south while Major General E. O. C. Ord's army hit him from the north. However, owing to an atmospheric freak condition, neither Ord nor Grant (who accompanied him) heard the sound of battle when Rosecrans assaulted Price on September 19. Consequently they did not attack, and Price, after beating off Rosecrans, slipped out of the trap that night.

Late in September Van Dorn came up from Vicksburg to join Price at Ripley, Mississippi. Taking command of their combined force of 22,000, he marched for Corinth, which was held by 23,000 Federals under Rosecrans. On October 3 he drove Rosecrans from his outer fortifications but the next day suffered hideous losses in an attempt to storm the town. A column sent by Grant blocked his retreat, but thanks to Armstrong's cavalry he managed to escape. Shortly after the battle a photographer took pictures of Texans killed assaulting a

Union redoubt known as Battery Robinette. They are among the most grim photos of the war. Any civilian viewing them would immediately realize that real-life—or rather real-death—battlefields bore little resemblance to the scenes depicted in Currier and Ives prints.

Bragg and Kirby Smith had expected swarms of recruits in Kentucky—indeed without them they could not hope to hold the state. Instead only about 2,500 joined their ragged legions. Disgusted, Bragg decided to resort to conscription. To that end he arranged for the installation of Richard C. Hawes as Confederate Governor of Kentucky. But the inauguration ceremonies, held at Frankfort, the state capital, on October 4, were abruptly terminated by Union shellfire. Buell had launched his counteroffensive—and sooner than Bragg had anticipated, with the result that he caught the Confederates badly scattered.

Bragg fell back, planning as he did so to regroup his units for a stand west of Lexington. However, on October 8, being pressed by advancing Federals near Perryville, he lashed back at them. Charging through sheets of cannon and rifle fire, 15,000 of Polk's and Hardee's veterans hurled back the Union line, which was held by 14,000 troops, many of them raw. Then, after being reinforced, the Northerners rallied, counterattacked, and regained much ground. Ferocious but indecisive fighting continued until nightfall. The Confederates lost 3,400 and the Federals 4,200 of the 22,000 men they had engaged.

Bragg thought that he faced at Perryville only a portion of Buell's army, most of which he believed heading for Lexington by way of Frankfort. In actuality Buell had threatened Frankfort with a small column of 7,000 while his main force, 54,000 strong, had advanced on Perryville. Furthermore, Bragg's assault fell on Buell's left wing alone. Fortunately for the Confederates, Buell was so far to the rear that he did not even know a battle was taking place until two hours after it started! And then, again through ignorance plus poor staff work, he failed to exploit a splendid opportunity to crush Polk's and Hardee's divisions by striking them in the flank and rear with his virtually unopposed center and right. In brief, both Bragg and Buell were lost in the fog of war.

That night Bragg, belatedly but in time, realized that he faced Buell's concentrated power at Perryville, whereas his and Kirby Smith's forces still were dispersed. He also learned of Van Dorn's debacle at Corinth, which meant that he could not expect any help from him but that Grant was free to aid Buell—or else sweep southward. Consequently he at once retreated, first to Harrodsburg, then to Bryantsville. There on October 12 he and Kirby Smith decided to return to Tennessee before the Federals cut them off from Cumberland Gap.

Twelve days later the last of the foot-sore Confederates trudged through Cumberland Gap on the way to Knoxville. Their invasion of Kentucky, like Lee's of Maryland the month before, had ended in failure after a brilliant beginning. Many Southerners then and afterward denounced Bragg for abandoning Kentucky without an all-out battle. Bragg, however, saw no point in risking his army fighting for the Confederate cause in the Bluegrass State when so few of the Kentuckians themselves were willing to fight for it.

Lincoln urged, indeed expected, Buell to follow the Confederates to Knoxville, defeat them, and liberate East Tennessee. Instead Buell headed for

Even larger camps of instruction like Camp Butler, near Cairo, Illinois, began to produce the regiments that would fight the western war. (ILLINOIS STATE HISTORICAL LIBRARY)

And in came the volunteers. The 52d Illinois paraded through Elgin, Illinois, on its way to put down rebellion. (ILLINOIS STATE HISTORICAL LIBRARY)

Nashville. Lincoln thereupon replaced him with Rosecrans—who completed the move to Nashville, then remained there through November and most of December despite repeated orders and even pleas from Washington to advance. Like Buell he believed that a winter invasion of mountainous, thinly populated East Tennessee would be logistically impractical and strategically barren. He preferred instead to accumulate a large stockpile of supplies before doing battle with Bragg, who in the meantime had shifted his forces—now and thereafter known as The Army of Tennessee—to Murfreesboro, thirty miles southeast of Nashville.

Both Buell and Rosecrans were not without justification in their concern about supplies. Late in December cavalry raids by Van Dorn and Forrest caused Grant to abandon an attempt to capture Vicksburg by marching south through Mississippi. Similarly Morgan and Wheeler snipped away at Rosecrans's communication lines in Tennessee and Kentucky, delaying thereby his preparations.

Finally, on the day after Christmas, Rosecrans moved out from Nashville with 45,000 troops and an immense wagon train containing twenty days' rations. Bragg waited for him west of Murfreesboro, his 40,000 men straddling easily fordable Stones River. The Federals arrived in front of the Confederate position on December 29, having been slowed by Wheeler's cavalry. Each commander made preparations to attack with his left. The only difference was that Bragg struck first. On the morning of December 31 the redoubtable southern infantry, spearheaded by Irish-born Patrick Cleburne's division, rolled back Rosecrans's right wing until it was at a 90-degree angle to his left. However, the Federals, whose defense was anchored by Irish-descended Phil Sheridan's division, managed to hold just short of the Nashville Pike, their lifeline to the north. A gallant but foolish Confederate attempt to break the Union center at the "Round Forest" failed and the mutual slaughter—for such it was—ceased with the coming of darkness.

That night Rosecrans asked his generals if he

should order a retreat. Bearlike George H. Thomas, awakened from a doze, said, "This army doesn't retreat," then went back to sleep. The army stood.

Both sides spent the first day of 1863 (the date the Emancipation Proclamation went into effect) recuperating and redeploying. Then on January 2 Bragg threw Breckinridge's division at Rosecrans's left. The blue infantry broke, but massed Federal artillery tore Breckinridge's ranks to pieces. During the night of January 3 Bragg, who had lost 10,000 men, retreated. Rosecrans did not pursue beyond Murfreesboro. He had suffered 13,000 casualties and Wheeler had destroyed many of his precious wagons. Although actually a draw, the battle was hailed as a victory in the North, where it revived morale that was flagging badly after Burnside's bloody fiasco at Fredericksburg.

Thus ended the first year of fighting in the West. Clearly the North had gained much, the South lost much. Indeed, it would scarcely be an exaggeration to say that while the South had been winning *battles* in the East, in the West the North had been winning the *war*.

But the western Confederates remained undaunted and dangerous. Union Colonel Abel D. Streight found this out the hard way. On April 11, 1863, he invaded Alabama with 1,500 mounted infantrymen, intending to destroy factories and railroads in North Georgia. Forrest, with 1,000 cavalry, pursued. Guided part of the way by sixteen-year-old Emma Sanson, who rode with him on his horse, he overtook Streight, harried him relentlessly, and finally captured his entire command on May 3.

Meanwhile Rosecrans's Army of the Cumberland, as it was now called, and Bragg's Army of Tennessee, lay motionless throughout the winter and spring, recuperating, skirmishing with cavalry, and steeling themselves for the fighting to come. That there would be more fighting—a great deal more—was obvious to all. It was just that no one knew when it would be, or where—although probably some general, gazing at the map, had already noted a stream, not far away in Georgia, with a strange name: Chickamauga, an Indian word meaning "River of Death."

Members of the 9th Missouri try to look their best on the street in St. Joseph, but these western soldiers will ever appear unkempt . . . and rugged as hell itself. (STATE HISTORICAL SOCIETY OF MISSOURI)

Friends and families saw them off to war in front of their courthouses, as here at Paris, Illinois, in April 1862. While the speeches were made and the colors presented, the wagons loaded with their gear awaited the march to Dixie. (LO)

From farther west they came by river steamer, like these Nebraska soldiers aboard the Henderson *at Bellview, Iowa, in 1861.* (NEBRASKA STATE HISTORICAL SOCIETY)

A troop transport loaded with soldiers lands at Cairo, Illinois, where the men will train for the war. These men come aboard the Aleck Scott, *unaware that before the war she was piloted briefly by a writer who will take his pen name from the cry of a steamboat leadsman, "Mark Twain." At the moment, he is still Samuel L. Clemens, and now a young and very scared Confederate soldier.* (10)

But these Confederates are not at all frightened. Officers all, their cigars and miniature flags proclaiming their bravado, they look forward to the coming fray. (LSU)

Southerners who remained loyal to the Union enjoyed wide popularity in the North, and often obtained high rank. Samuel P. Carter of East Tennessee outdid them all. A graduate of the United States Naval Academy, he was commissioned a brigadier general in the Army in 1862, simultaneously holding that rank and a commander's commission in the Navy. He was invaluable in stirring Union sentiment in Tennessee, and in 1862 was leading loyal Tennesseans in raids against their enemies. (NA)

The next month Confederates led by
Sterling Price besieged and captured
Lexington, Missouri, defended by
Colonel James A. Mulligan and his 23d
Illinois "Irish Brigade." (USAMHI)

By early 1862, Missouri still had not been
firmly taken by either side. On March
7–8, the largest battle west of the
Mississippi took place at Pea Ridge,
Arkansas, its outcome deciding the fate
of Missouri. Ben McCulloch would die
in the battle. Brigadier General
Alexander S. Asboth, leading a Union
division, would be wounded. (USAMHI)

Brigadier General Daniel M. Frost, a native of New York who sided with the South, was offered command of a brigade at Pea Ridge, but refused to accept such a small command and instead watched the battle "from a convenient height." (LSU)

Confederate Brigadier General Albert Pike was a native of Boston, Massachusetts, but raised Indian troops for the South in Arkansas and led them ingloriously at Pea Ridge. A fellow general said he was "either insane or untrue to the South." He resigned soon thereafter, and spent much of the rest of his life writing the ritual and dogma for Masonry. (NYHS)

Brigadier General William Y. Slack was mortally wounded on the first day at Pea Ridge and died two weeks later. It was nearly a month later that the Confederate Senate promoted him to brigadier, the news of his death not having reached them. The uniform in this photograph has been painted on. (VM)

A Confederate commander whose capabilities were as grand as his name, John Sappington Marmaduke. Educated at Yale and Harvard, he graduated from West Point in 1857, when this photograph was taken. Colonel of Missouri and Arkansas troops, he fought gallantly at Prairie Grove, Arkansas, in December 1862, and rose steadily in ability. He was the last Confederate to win promotion to major general, on March 18, 1865, and was later governor of Missouri. (LSU)

*While the war west of the
Mississippi dragged on in its bloody and
tragic course, one of the Union's first
victories came in January 1862 at Mill
Springs, Kentucky. Brigadier General
George H. Thomas, a native of Virginia,
led part of his division against the
Confederate command in southeast
Kentucky.* (USAMHI)

*Native of Kentucky, Brigadier General
James F. Fagan also distinguished
himself in the Confederate defeat at
Prairie Grove.* (JM)

The Confederates Thomas faced were
led by Major General George B.
Crittenden. His father was Senator
John J. Crittenden, who unsuccessfully
attempted a last-minute compromise
between North and South in 1861.
His brother was a major general in the
Union Army; so were Kentucky families
divided. This previously unpublished
photograph shows him probably in 1862.
He was forced to give battle to Thomas
at Mill Springs, thanks in part to
disobedience to his orders from a
subordinate . . . (LSU)

. . . Brigadier General Felix Zollicoffer
of Tennessee, who was killed when he
accidentally rode into Union troops
during the battle. (JM)

Mill Springs destroyed the right of the Confederate defensive line in Kentucky. Now a new general, Ulysses S. Grant, went to work on the left of the line. (USAMHI)

Assisted by Federal gunboats under the command of Flag Officer Andrew H. Foote, Grant moved against Confederate bastions on the Tennessee and Cumberland rivers. (LC)

Foote had four new river ironclads, among them the U.S.S. Cincinnati, *one of the powerful "city class" gunboats.* (NHC)

Another was the U.S.S. Carondelet, *heavily armed and armored, and here tied at the bank on one of the western rivers.* (NHC)

A markedly different ironclad was the U.S.S. Essex, *a converted centerwheel steamboat whose arming was personally overseen by her commander . . .* (USAMHI)

. . . William David Porter. Called "Dirty Bill" because of his unlikable manner and sometimes less-than-honest methods, he was the son of Commodore David Porter of the original Essex. *His brother was Admiral David D. Porter, his half-brother Admiral David Farragut. He would be badly scalded by steam when a shot from Confederate Fort Henry penetrated the* Essex's *boiler.* (USAMHI)

One of Foote's three wooden gunboats, the U.S.S. Tyler. *It would do workhorse duty on the western waters, though even great warships still had to dry their laundry now and then.* (USAMHI)

Grant and Foote first moved against Fort Henry on the Tennessee River. They set the attack for February 6, 1862, but mud slowed Grant's soldiers and it was all Foote's affair. He soon forced Confederate Brigadier General Lloyd Tilghman to lower his flag, after sending most of his garrison to Fort Donelson. (SHC)

Donelson would be a different matter entirely.
Commanding there was General John B. Floyd,
who a year before was Buchanan's Secretary
of War. On February 13, Grant launched his
land attack with the division of Brigadier General
Charles F. Smith, his one-time teacher at West
Point. (NA)

Two days later, facing a hopeless situation, Floyd
decided to escape, abandoning his command to
General Gideon J. Pillow. A man of reprehensible
character, Pillow, too, chose to flee rather than
share the fate of his soldiers. In January 1863,
at the Battle of Stones River, he would be seen
hiding behind a tree while his brigade went into
battle. Thereafter he gave perjured testimony
against fellow generals in the political infighting
that would always plague the Confederate Army
of Tennessee. (VM)

Others, too, won laurels. Benjamin Franklin Cheatham a brigadier from Tennessee, will be promoted to major general in recognition of his service at Shiloh. (MC)

Colonel James B. Walton ably commanded his . . . (THE HISTORIC NEW ORLEANS COLLECTION)

. . . Washington Artillery of New Orleans in the fight, the first for this branch of the famed organization that also sent several companies to the Virginia front. (CM)

Private John Rulle of the 2d Tennessee Infantry came to Shiloh ready for a fight, from the look of him. His unit were mostly Irishmen from Memphis. (HP)

The officers and noncommissioned officers of Captain A. M. Rutledge's Tennessee Battery, photographed on July 4, 1861. Their guns at Shiloh would severely discomfit the Federals. (TENNESSEE HISTORICAL SOCIETY)

*A magnificent photograph, taken May 10, 1861, of the "Clinch Rifles," men of
the 5th Georgia. The variety of clothing and pose, with their black servant in
the background, are among the most interesting to be found in Confederate
images. They were to be far less relaxed at Shiloh.* (JOSEPH CANOLE, JR.)

The peach orchard at Shiloh. Through here swarmed the Confederate corps of Brigadier General . . . (CHS)

. . . *John C. Breckinridge, formerly Vice-President and a presidential contender. No believer in secession, and almost certain that the Confederacy could not win, he was forced out of the Union and nevertheless took a command from President Davis.* (NA)

Breckinridge's corps and others were bottling up the Federal division of Brigadier General Benjamin M. Prentiss in a place called . . . (USAMHI)

. . . the Hornets' Nest. It was in one of their attacks that A. S. Johnston fell
mortally wounded. (CHS)

It was a bitter fight. Westerners like these used their Colt revolving rifles to deliver heavy fire power against the Confederates. (RP)

Brigadier General Daniel Ruggles, a native of Massachusetts, retaliated by massing some sixty-two cannon against the Hornets' Nest. (USAMHI)

In the final encirclement of Prentiss, Kentuckians of the Orphan Brigade closed the final trap. Colonel Thomas Hunt, standing eighth from the left here, commanded one of the Kentucky regiments that sealed the Federals' fate. (KHS)

More of the Kentuckians, photographed in August 1860, who would eventually man the Orphan Brigade. (KHS)

Finally Prentiss could not hold out longer, and beneath this tree he surrendered.
An early postwar photo. (CHS)

Meanwhile dour Major General Braxton
Bragg continually pushed the Federals
back toward the Tennessee River. (CM)

On the Federal right, Brigadier General
William T. Sherman, like Beauregard a
veteran of Bull Run, fell back under heavy
Confederate attacks. (USAMHI)

*Finally, as evening approached, a last line was established by Grant and
Sherman. These 24-pounder siege guns were a part of it, and here the Federals
stood.* (USAMHI)

*They held on stubbornly, men like Colonel Madison Miller of the 18th
Missouri.* (LC)

Men of the 7th Illinois Infantry, armed with their Henry repeating rifles.
(ILLINOIS STATE HISTORICAL LIBRARY)

Even bandsmen, usually noncombatants, took arms in holding the last line.
(CHICAGO PUBLIC LIBRARY, SPECIAL COLLECTIONS)

And boys like Johnny Clem, the "drummer boy of Shiloh," acted like men. (LC)

The arrival of a relief column under Brigadier General Don Carlos Buell late that evening finally ensured that Grant would not be pushed into the Tennessee. (USAMHI)

The next day, April 7, thanks to Buell's troops arriving here at Pittsburg Landing, and the exhaustion of the Confederates, Grant forced Beauregard to retire from the field. This photograph was taken a few days after the battle. The steamer at right is the Tycoon, *sent by the Cincinnati Sanitary Commission with stores and medical supplies for the wounded. Next to it is Grant's headquarters boat, the* Tigress. (USAMHI)

At right, the Universe *unloads more supplies for Grant's command. The*
Tigress *is at the center, and across the stream stands the wooden gunboat* Tyler.
*The guns from Foote's fleet played a large part in halting the Confederate drive
on April 6. Shiloh was not exactly a victory for Grant, but not a defeat either,
and in the aftermath of several Union disasters, that was more important.*
(USAMHI)

*Four days after Shiloh, Major General
Henry W. Halleck took command from
Grant. Called variously "Old Brains" and
"Old Wooden Head," he was an able
administrator, and a miserable general.
Outnumbering Beauregard two to one, he
still could not catch the Confederates at
Corinth.* (MJM)

Brigadier General Daniel Tyler, of Bull Run and Blackburn's Ford fame—or ill repute—was sent west to command a brigade in the "siege" that Halleck laid to Corinth. The Federals finally moved into the town the day after the enemy escaped them. (LC)

Later in the year, with a Federal command under Major General William S. Rosecrans stationed in and around Corinth, the Confederates were not so slow. Major General Sterling Price led his little army to Iuka on the way to Corinth, and was there attacked by Rosecrans on September 19. A previously unpublished portrait of Price in 1862. (TU)

Price's most trusted subordinate, Brigadier General Lewis Henry Little, was killed at Iuka while talking with Price by a bullet that first passed under Price's arm. (CHS)

Two weeks after Iuka, the armies collided again at Corinth, on October 3–4, 1862. (CHS)

It was an important railroad depot and supply center for Rosecrans and his growing army of 21,000 men. A Howard & Hull photograph taken before the battle. Their tent studio appears just left of the Tishomingo Hotel. (USAMHI)

Rosecrans's army were western men, men of the 47th Illinois . . . (WILLIAM M. ANDERSON)

. . . and the 2d Minnesota, which bore much of the brunt of the fighting.
(MHS)

*Their commander, Major General William
S. Rosecrans, was himself a western man,
born in Ohio. He is seen here, with a hint
of a smile, taken by Corinth photographer
George Armistead of Armistead & White,
sometime prior to the battle.* (LC)

*His opponent was the colorful Major
General Earl Van Dorn of Mississippi, the
loser at Pea Ridge.* (MISSISSIPPI
DEPARTMENT OF ARCHIVES & HISTORY)

*For two days they fought. The 8th Indiana Artillery was heavily engaged for
the Union.* (RP)

Fifty-two-year-old Brigadier General Thomas J. McKean led one of Rosecrans's divisions, even though he was considered too old for active command. He is seated here with members of his staff. (NYHS)

Samuel Jones, like many of these men in Mississippi in 1862, was another veteran of Bull Run. He commanded a division under Van Dorn, and was also in the process of making himself the second most photographed general of the Confederacy. (VM)

Major General Mansfield Lovell, a native of Washington, D.C., joined Van Dorn after he lost New Orleans to Farragut, and skillfully commanded the Confederate retreat from Corinth. (CHS)

It was a costly battle. Here in front of Federal Battery Robinette, the Confederate dead and their horses were piled deep. This photograph, taken the day after the battle, shows the horse of Colonel William P. Rogers in the center, and to the left of it, the body of Rogers himself. (WRHS)

*Several of the Confederate dead in front of Robinette. Colonel William P.
Rogers of the 2d Texas lies at left, and to his right, leaning on his shoulder, is
the body of Colonel W. H. Moore, who led a brigade of Missouri and
Mississippi troops in futile assaults against Robinette.* (ALABAMA STATE
DEPARTMENT OF ARCHIVES AND HISTORY)

The Confederate threat gone, Corinth became undisputedly a Union town, and the men of Rosecrans's army enjoyed it as they could. Supplies came in regularly, and Howard & Hall expanded their gallery next to the Tishomingo. (CHS)

Officers like Brigadier General Grenville Dodge established their headquarters in the better homes of the city. (CHS)

Life returned to normal for the inhabitants. (CHS)

The soldiers patronized the local business establishments. (CHS)

They built their winter quarters like Camp Davis, home for the 66th Illinois, south of the city. (ROBERT YOUNGER)

Their bands tuned for the season's demands for entertainments. Here the 97th Indiana musicians. (CHS)

And their earthworks and tents dotted the landscape for the winter ahead,
while the firms of Armistead & White and Howard & Hall kept busy with their
captive clientele. Winter quarters could mean a small fortune to a
photographer. (CHS)

But it would not be a peaceful winter in
Mississippi and Tennessee, nor in
Kentucky. Brigadier General Jefferson C.
Davis, once an officer in Fort Sumter, in
late September shot and killed his superior,
William Nelson, after an altercation. It
could not have come at a worse time, for
after a year of seeming security, Kentucky
was being invaded by the Confederate
Army of Tennessee, commanded now by
Beauregard's successor . . . (LC)

. . . *General Braxton Bragg. This previously unpublished image of Bragg was made by McIntyre of Montgomery, Alabama, just a few weeks prior to his launching of the Kentucky campaign.* (CM)

Commanding the Federals who would resist Bragg was Major General Don Carlos Buell, of Shiloh. (USAMHI)

Bragg's offensive was spearheaded by a Floridian, Major General Kirby Smith, who had been wounded leading a brigade at Bull Run. At Richmond, Kentucky, he defeated Nelson in the only real Confederate battle victory of the campaign. (LC)

Leading Bragg's cavalry was a young brigadier who turned twenty-six during the campaign, Joseph Wheeler. He would become one of the war's premier cavalrymen. (LC)

Bragg and Buell finally met at Perryville, Kentucky, along Doctor's Creek. Probably an early postwar view. (USAMHI)

The H. P. Bottoms House near the position of Brigadier General Lovell Rousseau, who gallantly led a division against repeated enemy attacks. (USAMHI)

Rousseau aligned his command beside a 100-year-old tree that, miraculously, survived the battle. (USAMHI)

Federal artillery placed on this high ground, plus numerical superiority, finally gave the battle to Buell. (USAMHI)

Brigadier General J. Patton Anderson of Tennessee led one of Bragg's divisions to no avail. (USAMHI)

Losses were heavy. General S. A. M. Wood took a serious wound from Federal fire. (VM)

Union Brigadier General William R. Terrill of Virginia was struck in the side by a piece of shell and died that night. His brother was a general in the Confederate Army, and would die in the war as well. (USAMHI)

Brigadier General James S. Jackson was a native of Kentucky, and at Perryville he died on his home soil. (USAMHI)

Heavy fighting along this lane cost Buell even more casualties, but the battle was his. (USAMHI)

Bragg watered his army at this spring, and retreated into Tennessee, his dream of conquering Kentucky gone in smoke. (USAMHI)

In December the armies meet again, this time at Murfreesboro, Tennessee, and the Federals are once again commanded by Major General William S. Rosecrans. He is seated fourth from the left in this pose with his staff. The man sitting next to him on the right is Brigadier General James A. Garfield, who will become his chief of staff after the battle and, years later, President of the United States. To the far right sits Philip H. Sheridan who, as a brigadier, commands a division at Murfreesboro, and wins promotion. (USAMHI)

The courthouse in Murfreesboro. The town remained in Confederate hands during the battle. (USAMHI)

The telegraph office from which Bragg boastfully—and prematurely—wired President Davis that he had won a great victory. (USAMHI)

Rosecrans fought a largely defensive battle, letting Bragg hurl his divisions against tough fighters like the 38th Indiana, shown here in Murfreesboro in April 1863. (JMB)

Those attacks were overseen by Bragg's corps commanders. Lieutenant General William J. Hardee of Georgia was known widely in both armies, thanks to his authorship of Hardee's Tactics, a standard manual North and South. (LC)

Lieutenant General Leonidas Polk of North Carolina commanded Bragg's other corps. Episcopal Missionary Bishop for the Southwest, he traded clerical robes for a uniform when the war came. He would disappoint almost everyone. (VM)

Some of the greatest infantry assaults of the war took place at Murfreesboro, and they were terribly bloody. Brigadier General Roger Hanson of Kentucky, commander of the Orphan Brigade, fell mortally wounded when the fuse from an exploding shell struck his leg. While being carried from the field he cheered his men, telling them that it was a glorious cause to die for. (JM)

Brigadier General James E. Rains was killed leading his division of Hardee's corps into a charge. His last word was "Forward!" (USAMHI)

Determined resistance by Sheridan and others finally forced Bragg to abandon the field and retreat into the interior, leaving the Federals the field and the victory. (USAMHI)

The Federals occupied Murfreesboro for most of the rest of the war. Here the headquarters from which Rosecrans sent Lincoln the good news of a victory for the New Year, 1863. (USAMHI)

Photographer of the Confederacy: J. D. Edwards

LESLIE D. JENSEN

Prolific yet unknown chronicler of rustics in rebellion

BEFORE the war guns really roared, East or West, on May 14, 1861, the citizens of New Orleans, reading the military columns of their newspapers, came across the following advertisement:

THE WAR!

Views of Pensacola, Forts Barancas, McRae and Pickens; of the Companies there— "Orleans Cadets" "Crescent Rifles" "Chausseurs a Pied," Mississippi and Alabama Regiments and of the U.S. Fleet—39 different Photographic Views, taken by an accomplished artist on the spot, will be on sale tomorrow at the Book Stores, Picture and Looking Glass Stores. They are very large and taken superbly. Price $1 per copy.

The "accomplished artist" was J. D. Edwards, a shadowy figure who remains obscure to this day, yet a man who had accomplished a feat that would not be repeated in the Confederacy. Edwards had produced a comprehensive photographic panorama of the forts, guns, barracks, shipyards, and most importantly, the men who comprised the Confederate Army. Were it not for Edwards, photographic coverage of Confederate military events

would be limited to a mere handful of isolated pictures, many of them taken in northern prison camps.

Little is known about Edwards personally or of his life before his Pensacola views went on sale, and practically nothing is known of him afterward. In 1860, he was working in New Orleans. Edwards was twenty-nine years old at the time, had been born in New Hampshire, and gave his occupation as "Ambrotype Portrait." His wife, Mary, a Missourian by birth, was twenty. The Edwardses could not have been in New Orleans long, for their son Edouard had been born in Massachusetts only eight months before. The remainder of the household consisted of Eliza Zeigler, a nineteen-year-old German servant, and Edwards's two assistants, B. Barker, a twenty-nine-year-old native of Massachusetts, and a twenty-four-year-old Canadian named Johnson. Edwards valued his personal estate at $3,000.

Yet, though a newcomer to New Orleans, Edwards must have made an impression of being innovative and willing to take on unusual business assignments. When the U. S. Treasury Department and Custom House and the Marine Hospital were under construction in June 1860, Edwards took twenty-three views of the former and twelve views of the latter for the U. S. Army Engineer in charge of the work, a native Louisianan named P. G. T. Beauregard. This assignment may well have started a tradition for both men, outdoor photography for Edwards, and the inclusion of photographs with reports for Beauregard, a practice he continued during the 1861 and 1863 Charleston operations.

By 1861, Edwards operated a studio at 23 Royal Street, yet, though he was listed in the alphabetical section of a city directory, he was still not established enough to be included in the separate section devoted to photographers. Later in the year he moved to 19 Royal Street, occupied when the directory was put out by a photographer named E. J. Newton, Jr. It is not known whether Edwards bought out Newton's operation or went into business with him.

After the firing on Fort Sumter, only one major U.S. bastion remained in the Confederacy: Fort Pickens, guarding the harbor of Pensacola Bay, Florida. The importance of Fort Pickens has often been overshadowed by other events, and particularly because no major battles were fought to control it. Yet, in April 1861, it was one of the most important areas of potential trouble. As the last Union stronghold on Confederate soil, it was not only irritating to southern pride, but it blocked the bay to southern shipping and restricted the use of the splendid former U. S. Navy Yard at Warrington, just across the bay from the fort. Moreover, it could, and in time did, become a base for operations against the Confederacy. Whoever controlled Fort Pickens controlled the use of one of the best anchorages on the Gulf Coast.

Theoretically, the Confederates, vastly outnumbering the Union troops in the area, should have had little trouble taking control of the bay, but the unexpected stubbornness of Lieutenant Adam Slemmer's tiny Union command, supported by an ever growing Union fleet, kept the Confederates at bay until Union reinforcements arrived. By late April, Confederate volunteers poured into the area, preparing for what everyone thought would be the next big showdown of the war. Many of the Confederates headed for Pensacola were from New Orleans, and J. D. Edwards apparently saw in this an opportunity to create a pictorial record of the war, make a reputation for himself, and turn a profit by selling his products to the soldiers and the folks back home. Accordingly, sometime in late April, he too headed for the scene of the war's next battle.

Happily, because Edwards numbered at least some of his negatives in the order he took them, it is possible to follow his work pattern in the Pensacola area with a fair degree of certainty. He seems to have started at the Navy Yard itself, where General Braxton Bragg had his headquarters and where Edwards probably had to go to get permission to take his photographs. He took pictures looking across the bay toward Fort Pickens and photographed the steamer *Fulton* in dry dock, surrounded by the vast quantities of shells the Confederates had both captured and were making in the yard's foundry. From there, he moved west, photographing Coppens's Louisiana Zouave Battalion at drill on the grounds of the Marine Barracks. He spent a great deal of time at Fort Barrancas, photographing it inside and out, including its old Spanish half-moon battery. From there, Edwards photographed some of the sand batteries and then found himself drawn to the lighthouse. Its 165-foot height provided a perfect view of the coast, and Edwards took his camera to the top, photographing the forts and camps below. He spent considerable time in the camps themselves, mostly in those of the 1st Alabama and 9th Mississippi regiments, before moving on to the Confederate bastion on the right flank, Fort McRee. On the way back, Edwards may have taken additional camp scenes, and at some point, probably toward the end of his stay, he went to Bayou Grand, just north of Warrington, where he photographed the camp of the Orleans Cadets. Exactly how long Edwards stayed in the Pensacola area is unknown, but given the volume of work that he did and the probable work and travel time, he may have been there a week or more.

The photographs went on sale in New Orleans on May 15, but curiously, Edwards only ran his notice for three days. The various newspapers made some editorial comment on the photographs, but beyond confirming that the advertisement indeed refers to the work of J. D. Edwards, they tell us little. The New Orleans *Bee,* however, suggested that the photographs would "make an interesting souvenir for the parlor, particularly in the event, considered now so near at hand, of the capture of Fort Pickens."

Some of the photographs made their way north with surprising speed. On June 15, a woodcut appeared in *Harper's Weekly* entitled "INTERIOR OF A SAND-BAG BATTERY BEARING ON FORT PICKENS." *Harper's* claimed that it was the work of their special artist, Theodore Davis, but close comparison with Edwards's photograph No. 33, "Perote Sand Batteries 10 inch Columbiads," reveals the woodcut to have been pirated from Edwards. It is entirely possible that Davis, who had been in Pensacola with William Howard Russell at about the time Edwards was photographing, knew Edwards's work and either made a sketch from the photograph or simply sent the photograph on to *Harper's,* who incorrectly captioned it. A week later, *Harper's* ran another woodcut with the caption "BIVOUAC OF REBEL TROOPS AT GENERAL BRAGG'S CAMP AT WARRINGTON, FLORIDA," and this time admitted that it was from a photograph, although they did not identify the photographer. The scene was the well-known one of men cooking around a campfire in the 9th Mississippi's camp, but *Harper's,* not content with the original photograph, rearranged the figures.

Edwards's photographs seem to have been rather widely distributed at the time. Some ended up in the hands of S. H. Lockett, an officer in the 1st Alabama, and somehow Charles Allgower, a member of the 6th New York and an occasional artist for *Harper's,* also acquired some, probably while his regiment was stationed in the Pensacola area. Despite Edwards's claim that he produced thirty-nine views, it is now clear that the actual total was much higher. Known views, many of them published in 1911 but since lost, total forty-four. However, Edwards's negative numbers run as high as sixty-eight, and there is at least one photograph numbered "2B." Thus, despite the large number of Edwards photographs which are presented here for the first time, there may be as many as twenty or more yet unaccounted for, including at least two, those of the Crescent Rifles and the Chausseurs à Pied, referred to in the ad.

One wonders whether the appearance of the woodcuts in *Harper's Weekly* may have been a spur to another photographer, the nation's finest, Mathew B. Brady. The Confederates had already scooped him in the early coverage of the war, and the fact that their photographs were appearing in northern papers, competing with his own portrait work, may well have helped to inspire Brady to take his camera teams into the field.

The fact that the Pensacola front never produced any major battles and was eventually abandoned by the Confederates may have hurt the long-term sales of Edwards's work, but in any case, after the appearance of the photographs, he slipped once more into obscurity. Two of his negatives were seized by U.S. authorities after the fall of New Orleans, and prints from them were turned over to the U. S. Engineers office in Washington in 1863. Unfortunately, we do not know the circumstances of the seizure, and while the prints survive, the negatives have disappeared. Francis Trevelyan Miller claimed that Edwards later worked for the Confederate secret service, but no hard evidence to support the claim has come to light. Yet, there is one tantalizing clue which may indicate that Edwards was an even more important photographer than his Pensacola series indicates. Roy M. Mason, one of the searchers sent by Miller to locate Confederate photographs for the 1911 *Photographic History of the Civil War,* recalled his experiences in the armory of the Washington Artillery in New Orleans. He noted that the one-armed armorer, Sergeant Dan Kelly, "said that there were no photographs, but consented to look in the long rows of dusty shelves which line the sides of the huge, dark armory. From almost the last he drew forth a pile of soggy, limp cardboard, covered with the grime of years. He passed his sleeve carelessly over the first, and there spread into view a picture of his father sitting reading among his comrades in Camp Louisiana forty-nine years before. The photographs were those of J. D. Edwards, who had also worked at Pensacola and Mobile. Here were Confederate volunteers of '61 and the boys of the Washington Artillery which became so famous in the service of the Army of Northern Virginia." Some Washington Artillery photos were by J. W. Petty of New Orleans, but if Mason's implication is correct, Edwards may have continued to photograph Confederate troops at least as late as early 1862, when the 5th Company, Washington Artillery was photographed just before Shiloh. If so, Edwards may be responsible for a larger body of Confederate photographs than he has been given credit for.

Yet, if early 1862 was the last time that Edwards may have been at work, it is also the end of any documentation on him. The man simply disappeared. He turns up in no postwar New Orleans directories and efforts to trace him back north have proved futile. We know nothing of his subsequent career, indeed, we do not even know when or where he died.

Miller called Edwards a "pioneer camera man," but apparently even Miller was not aware of just how much of a pioneer Edwards was. In this country there was virtually no tradition of war photography, and while the Crimean War photographs of Roger Fenton and others were known, there was no one who could set the pace in this new art. While enterprising Confederates in Charleston were the first on the scene of America's bloodiest war, their job was made easier by the fact that they were photographing local events. The established photographers remained in their studios, content to take the portraits of the generals and soldiers who would fight the war. Into this scene stepped J. D. Edwards, packing his equipment over miles of swamps and bayous and into a war zone, taking pictures at least as good as Brady's and then marketing them with little apparent financial backing other than his own. At the time Edwards's work was of a far wider scope than anything any other photographer was producing, and while he was eclipsed by the superior resources of Brady, Gardner, and hundreds of others, it was J. D. Edwards, whether known by name to these other photographers or not, who showed the way a war could be photographed. In the Confederacy, no one else would match his work for innovation and sheer importance. If there was anyone who could claim the title Photographer of the Confederacy, it was the obscure Yankee from New Orleans, J. D. Edwards.

With only four exceptions, all of the J. D. Edwards photographs reproduced here are published for the first time. Several others were published in 1911, but the originals from which they were reproduced have since disappeared. The images that follow are all taken from surviving original prints newly unearthed.

The ever-frowning brow of General Braxton Bragg. He commanded the regiments of rustics forming at Pensacola when Edwards made his historic visit in April 1861. (CHS)

First Lieutenant Adam J. Slemmer of the 1st United States Artillery, the thorn in Bragg's side who refused to give up Fort Pickens, thus ensuring the mighty bastion for the Union as a base deep in Confederate territory. Edwards never captured Slemmer as Cook did Major Anderson and his men at Fort Sumter, but more than once he turned his camera toward the low, brooding profile of Pickens, a constant reminder of Federal power and determination. (USAMHI)

Fort Pickens photographed from Fort Barrancas, across Pensacola Harbor. The ship is probably the Federal flag-of-truce boat U.S.S. Wyandotte. (SHC)

Guns in the old Spanish part of Fort Barrancas, trained on Fort Pickens in the distance. "I was rather interested with Fort Barrancas," wrote William H. Russell, "built by the Spaniards long ago—an old work on the old plan, weakly armed, but possessing a tolerable command from the face of fire." (SHC)

The rear of Fort Barrancas and a Confederate regiment camped beyond, probably the 1st Alabama. The variety of tents, the makeshift nature of the camp, and lack of uniformity in the dress of the Confederates drawn up in line, all attest to the informal and inexperienced nature of the Southrons who flocked to Pensacola in 1861. (GULF ISLANDS NATIONAL SEASHORE)

*A side view of part of Fort Barrancas as Bragg's men move yet another cannon
into place.* (SHC)

A water battery at Warrington. In the distance to the right is the lighthouse. Bragg did not wish to open fire on Pickens, and the Englishman Russell believed him right. "The magazines of the batteries I visited did not contain ammunition for more than one day's ordinary firing," he wrote. "The shots were badly cast, with projecting flanges from the mould, which would be very injurious to soft metal guns in firing." One of these rustics, standing at the wheel of the front gun, holds a shot in his hand, while his mates sham preparing to fire. The poor man at the second gun, seeing his chance for immortality about to be blocked by a cold iron cannon, had to stoop to present his face to the camera. In the right center is a hot-shot furnace for heating incendiary projectiles. (NA, OFFICE OF THE CHIEF OF ENGINEERS)

The sand battery at Fort Barrancas, and a stand of the ill-formed shot. Despite the seemingly strong positions of these guns, Russell believed that if Bragg opened fire on Slemmer, Fort Pickens "ought certainly to knock his works about his ears." (SHC)

Edwards captioned this a "View of two Sand Batteries, showing subterranean passages connecting them together, with Fort Pickens in the distance." Pickens has now disappeared from this faded print, but the crude board shoring of the tunnels is visible in the foreground. Much work remains to be done, but Russell did not find the summer soldiers anxious about it. "The working parties, as they were called—volunteers from Mississippi and Alabama, great long-bearded fellows in flannel shirts and slouched hats, uniformless in all save brightly burnished arms and resolute purpose—were lying about among the works, or contributing languidly to their completion." (TU)

The lighthouse west of Fort Barrancas. Built in 1859, it quickly attracted Edwards's eye, and he and his camera were soon at its top taking the first "aerial" photos of the war. (PENSACOLA HISTORICAL SOCIETY, PENSACOLA, FLORIDA)

Looking east from the lighthouse. Barely visible on the shore in the right center is a two-gun sand battery. Just above the right-hand row of tents is another. And just above the tents at left, distinguishable by the straight horizontal line of its parapet, is Fort Barrancas. The buildings to its left are the Barrancas Barracks, while the tall building with cupola in the distance to the right of the barracks is the Marine Hospital. This is, arguably, the first "aerial" photograph in military history. (SHC)

Confederate camps and a four-gun sand battery immediately below the lighthouse. The "subterranean passages" connecting the guns are clearly visible, as are several Confederates lounging in the vicinity. These are Alabama troops. In the distance on the low spit of sand dune is Fort McRee, "weak and badly built," thought Russell, and "quite under the command of Pickens." (GULF ISLANDS NATIONAL SEASHORE)

*A Confederate encampment just south of Bayou Grande, near Pensacola,
probably the Orleans Cadets. This may be the finest Confederate camp scene to
survive, excellent not only for its clarity, but for what it shows as well. Almost
every aspect of camp life is depicted. A bugler with his instrument to his lips, a
soldier with fishing pole in hand, men reading letters and newspapers, others
cleaning their rifles, a fatigue detail with shovel on shoulder, two Johnnies
feigning a spar, and at right, pipe in mouth, a company officer handing orders
to a saluting corporal. To the left are piled boxes of fresh rations. In this image
Edwards outdid himself.* (STATE PHOTOGRAPHIC ARCHIVES, STROZIER LIBRARY,
FLORIDA STATE UNIVERSITY)

The encampment of the Louisville Blues, the 1st Alabama, near the lighthouse. There is a definite lack of order in this camp, blankets and clothing and equipment hanging wherever convenient. These men would learn a lot about soldiering in the years ahead, and about sanitation, too. A trench, perhaps a latrine, is just a few feet to the left of their tents and mess area. Disease, in this war, will kill far more men than bullets. (RP)

Camps of Mississippi regiments behind the lighthouse. (TU)

*Edwards did not move his camera after capturing the Mississippi camps.
Instead, he moved the Mississippians. Here they parade in all their sartorial
chaos. Top hats, stovepipes, slouch and military caps, hunting shirts, bow ties,
flannel checks, and their captain in front in a decidedly unmilitary vest. Yet
they all have rifles, and an unshakable determination. Nowhere in the world
was there another soldiery like them.* (PHS)

*The 9th Mississippi in camp, and for an Edwards photo, an unusually clear
surviving print. Rarely can one see such a brilliant representation of the
Confederate soldier of 1861. Especially eye-catching is the soldier crouching to
the left of the stand of rifles at left. The significance of the numeral "4" on his
shirt is unknown, but his resplendence is unarguable. They all have the lean,
hardened look of the American backwoods. Such men could be unbeatable.* (RP)

*Fifth Avenue, looking north from the southeast corner of Twenty-eighth Street,
New York, 1865.* (NYHS)

important gain since wool offered the most common substitute for the cotton supply diminished by the South's secession.

Apparently photographers, like other Northerners, took great pride in this record of productivity; at least they delighted in capturing scenes showing the new machines at work. But when they turned their attention to the factories, something more than productivity caught the eye. Pictures of giant machines sweeping across fields, or of fishing boats plying the waters of Nantucket, conveyed a sense of majesty, even charm. However, scenes of women and small children toiling in a factory, although they might suggest the sacrifice and pro-

ductivity so vital to the war effort, were utterly lacking in beauty or nobility. Unlike the sight of a man or woman astride a reaper, no charm attached to the spectacle of people young and old harnessed to machines inside dingy mills.

But the mills and factories played a major role in carrying the North to victory. From their bustling, clanging interiors came a swelling stream of muskets, cannon, equipment, locomotives, rails, wagons, tools, uniforms, shoes, and thousands of other items. Wartime needs spurred the development of other industries besides agricultural implements and armaments. The demand for uniforms and shoes prompted increased use of sewing machines. One by-product of this work was the discovery that uniforms and shoes manufactured in a few basic sizes would fit most men. This standardization simplified the production of uniforms and shoes in quantity and after the war stimulated the rise of the ready-made clothing industry. Military needs also lent a strong impetus to the canned food industry, including Gail Borden's canned milk. The desire to produce canned food quickly and in quantity led to improvements in canning techniques and machinery.

As its farms and factories responded to the war effort, an aura of prosperity settled across the North. Newspapers and politicians alike waxed elo-

quent over the nation's material well-being. The New York *Times* noted in 1864 that Northerners were better housed, clothed, and fed than ever before "in the midst of the most gigantic civil war . . . yet seen." Wholesale farm prices doubled during the war years while nonagricultural wages rose 43 per cent. Farm land values soared, as did real estate values in general.

For most Northerners, however, this prosperity proved more apparent than real. As always, wartime brought a sharp inflationary trend which in many cases erased gains in wages or income. Wholesale prices more than doubled while the consumer price index increased from 102 to 177. Ac-

Chestnut Street in Philadelphia just before the war. Hotels, booksellers, typesetters, engravers—the North bustled with the work of tradesmen and artisans. (FREE LIBRARY OF PHILADELPHIA)

Away from the eastern coast, the market towns and county seats continued to thrive as before the conflict. Indeed, the presence of large-scale armies boosted business in many communities. The market square in Carlisle, Pennsylvania, in 1862. (LC)

cording to one recent calculation, the real wage index actually declined from 102 in January 1861 to 67 in January 1865.

Wage earners suffered most from the ravages of inflation, but attempts to improve their lot through organization made little headway during the war. Most wartime trade unions began at the local level, primarily in New York, Pennsylvania, and Massachusetts, and boasted some 300 locals with an estimated 200,000 members by 1865. City federations, begun in Rochester in March 1863, soon sprang up in most major industrial centers. Intended only as advisory bodies, the federations as-

sumed such tasks as organizing trades and boycotts, generating publicity during strikes, and opposing the importation of strikebreakers. They also founded labor newspapers and in thirty-six cities and towns helped establish cooperative stores.

Attempts to revive national trade associations made some gains, but the national organizations were loose bodies with little effective power over their locals. In general the labor movement remained weak during the war. Unskilled workers, especially women, children, and blacks, endured starvation wages and sweatshop conditions with little hope of improving their lot.

Hanover Junction, Pennsylvania, around November 1863. Like hundreds of minor railroad towns, its townspeople saw little of the war and felt its effects even less, except when the trains came through loaded with soldiers going to the front. (USAMHI)

Wartime conditions imposed unusual hardships upon workers. According to a Senate report, industrial workers provided the Union Army with about one third of its troops. The Conscription Act of 1863, with its provision that service might be evaded by hiring a substitute or paying a three-hundred-dollar commutation fee, especially rankled laborers. On several occasions resentment against the draft boiled into bloody riots. The most spectacular of these occurred in New York City in July 1863 when a mob wrecked the recruiting station, demolished rail and streetcar lines and shipyards, closed factories, attacked the homes of leading Republicans, and killed several blacks. Similar riots engulfed other cities in turmoil but brought no relief to workers.

Strikes proved equally futile in wartime. The public regarded them as disloyal and the government sometimes responded with troops. On several occasions President Lincoln felt obliged to inter-

vene in an attempt to salve the feelings of workers and preserve their loyalty to the war effort. At the same time the government took steps to increase the labor supply diminished by military service and a decline in immigration. In both 1861 and 1862 immigration, which had averaged 281,455 people a year during the 1850s, fell off to slightly less than 92,000. The figure rose to 176,282 in 1863, but the following year Congress, prodded by Lincoln and concerned industrialists, passed a law which permitted the importation of contract laborers. Whatever the effect of this act, immigration rose to 193,418 in 1864 and 248,120 in 1865.

But if workers found prosperity elusive, many businessmen reaped fat profits from wartime opportunities. Alert contractors were quick to take advantage of the government's needs. Some were content to earn legitimate fortunes while others resorted to dishonest means to make their killings. Never had the nation created so large an army or required armaments and equipment on so vast a scale. The scale of operations, as well as the urgency of purchasing so much so quickly, invited corruption of unprecedented dimensions. Revelation after revelation rocked the public, prompting the New York *Herald* in June 1864 to denounce the "gross corruption prevailing in nearly every department of the government." Large commissions went to men whose only service was to procure lucrative government contracts for firms.

On the stock and gold exchanges, speculators thrived on the uncertainties of wartime. Good news from the front boosted the prices of gold and stocks; bad news sent them crashing downward. Hordes of speculators, including some women braving ridicule in a traditionally male arena, plunged into the treacherous currents of Wall Street seeking a quick fortune. One crafty manipulator, Daniel Drew, recalled that "Along with ordinary happenings, we fellows in Wall Street had the fortunes of war to speculate about. . . . It's good

An apple seller in Cincinnati, Ohio, typical of the street vendors that every large city spawned. (LO)

fishing in troubled waters." Young Jay Gould went one step further: he devised an ingenious system whereby he obtained by telegraph advance information on Union victories or defeats and shifted his speculations accordingly.

Not all northern businessmen were corrupt or dishonest, and not all made fortunes. But the war created a free-wheeling, opportunistic atmosphere that proved irresistible to many people. It is important to remember that not all Northerners bothered to fight the war or even tender it active support. Some people lacked strong interest in the conflict and either ignored it as best they could or resented it as an intrusion into their private affairs.

Among this group were men who found the wartime situation a golden opportunity for self-advancement. Their activities escaped the camera's eye, as did those of the plungers on Wall Street and the hustlers of government contracts, but their ultimate importance rivaled anything that took place on the battlefield. These ambitious young entrepreneurs used the war years to establish themselves in business while their peers were caught up in the clash of arms. Some made their fortunes even before the war ended, while others planted the roots of what were to be long and prosperous careers.

Within this group could be found a surprising number of the business titans who were to dominate the economy, and therefore much of American life, during the half century between the Civil War and World War I: Andrew Carnegie, J. P. Morgan, John D. Rockefeller, George F. Baker, James J. Hill, Gustavus Swift, Charles A. Pillsbury, George M. Pullman, Mark Hanna, Marshall Field, Jay Gould, John Wanamaker, and Peter Widener, to name but a few. Each of these men, and others like them, ignored the call to arms and concentrated instead upon the windfall business opportunities bred by wartime conditions. Few of them even tried to enlist, fewer still stayed home because of disability, and several (Carnegie, Gould, Morgan, Rockefeller, and Philip D. Armour among them) hired substitutes.

In later years some of these men grew defensive about their failure to enter the service. "I was represented in the army," Rockefeller insisted. "I sent more than twenty men, yes, nearly thirty. That is, I made such arrangements for them that they were able to go." The majority, however,

*St. Paul, Minnesota, a city that grew largely from the speculations in the 1850s
of Washington politicians and bankers, several of them now Confederates.* (MHS)

seemed content to concentrate on the business at hand. One son of banker Thomas Mellon begged his father for money to speculate in wheat. Writing from Wisconsin, he observed that people "continue growing richer and don't care when the war closes." Mindful of the educational value afforded by prevailing conditions, the elder Mellon flatly forbade another son from enlisting:

I had hoped my boy was going to make a smart intelligent businessman and was not such a goose as to be *seduced from duty* by the declamations of buncombe speeches. It is only greenhorns who enlist. *You can learn nothing in the army.* . . . In time you will come to understand and believe that a man may be a patriot without risking his own life or sacrificing his health. There are plenty of other lives less valuable or ready to serve for the love of serving.

To most of these men, wartime opportunities brought financial nest eggs from which huge fortunes later hatched. For them, and for many others

who advanced their prospects during those turbulent years, prosperity was anything but illusory.

Social activities reflected this mood of rising affluence, especially in the cities. As the war dragged on through month after weary month of bloody battles that produced defeat or indecision, Northerners sought diversions to dispel the gloom of uncertainty that clouded the future. So frenetic did the quest for amusement and gaiety become that stern observers periodically denounced the populace for their indifference to the suffering and hardships endured by soldiers at the front.

In rural areas, where the workday was always long and sources of amusement few, life went on much as it had before the war. There were church socials, husking bees, country fairs, and occasional barn dances. Young men played baseball or competed in foot races, wrestling, and shooting matches. A religious revival or camp meeting, accompanied by picnics and other festivities, might enliven a farm community for a week or more. Many a small town possessed an "opry house" that never saw an opera but welcomed touring lectures, dramatic companies, or minstrel shows. Occasionally too a traveling circus might wend its way through the countryside, thrilling farm folk with its menagerie of strange animals and exotic freaks. No event rivaled the celebration of national holidays like the Fourth of July, for which families gathered from miles around to enjoy barbeques, games, fireworks, oratory, and dancing, usually accompanied by liberal swigs from jugs of whiskey or hard cider.

City life offered far more varied and sophisticated amusements. As always the upper class set the standards and indulged themselves most freely. Dinners, receptions, and elegant parties occupied the fashionable in every city, especially Washington and New York. Roller-skating made its appearance in 1863 and New York's social denizens seized upon it as a pleasure which they hoped to confine to "the educated and refined classes." Ice-skating parties lightened the tedium of winter while periodic visits to fashionable resorts in Newport, Narragansett Pier, or upstate New York helped pass the summer months. Every major city had its lyceums and lecture halls, and in New York the Academy of Music offered the cultured elite a sampling of grand opera imported from Europe.

Crowds flocked to the theaters of every city in unprecedented numbers. Comedies were the staple fare, both in the high-tone playhouses and in lower-class theaters like those in New York's Bowery, where huge crowds gathered to yell and whistle, cheer and hiss, chew peanuts and spit tobacco juice. Although the emphasis upon comedy reflected a desire to escape the war, at least for a few hours, dramas based upon recent battles also proved popular. One energetic producer opened a play about Bull Run within a month of the battle, and later engagements were put on the boards by adapting a standard script to each occasion.

Besides theater, northern urbanites patronized minstrel shows, burlesque, dance halls, winter gardens, prizefights, cockfights, and the saloons. In New York, P. T. Barnum's American Museum drew enormous crowds, as did imitation counterparts in other cities. To the rest of the North Barnum sent his traveling circus, the Grand Colossal Museum and Menagerie, with curiosities borrowed from the American Museum and animals gathered from every corner of the world.

As always in wartime, amusements offered a counterpoint to anxiety and uncertainty. To out-

ward appearance, at least as the photographer captured it, life in the North hewed as closely to its normal patterns as was possible in an era of great duress. The camera recorded with an unblinking eye scenes of a wartime society clinging to its familiar habits while adjusting to changes imposed by the conflict. In so doing it portrayed the landscape of northern society unembellished and often unadorned. This fidelity freed later generations from the illustrator's imagination. Unlike the artist's drawing, the photograph offered viewers not an interpretation of a scene but some raw materials of a scene which one might interpret for himself.

More than this the camera could not do. For one thing the technology of photography was still in its infancy. Photographers still relied upon the wet-plate collodion process, a cumbersome and complicated business which required a wagonload of equipment, including a traveling dark tent for immediate developing, for all work done outside the studio. In effect the photographer could not operate abroad without carrying his laboratory with him. Even then he could not take action pictures with the equipment at his disposal.

In a real sense, then, the camera could capture little more than the bare surface of northern life during the war. On one hand, most of what was important took place beyond the photographer's—or anyone else's—eye; on the other, the technology of photography was unprepared to record the dynamism that was the essence of life in the North during these years.

War is not a still life, either on the battlefield or on the home front. The camera could preserve the residue of battle but not battle itself, the portraits of heroes but not their heroic deeds. Similarly, it might depict the stage, scenery, and characters of northern life, but not the dramatic action or inner moods and conflicts of the play itself. That realm still belonged to the writers, the painters, and the illustrators.

It is not possible to reconstruct the North at war through photographs or any other artifacts. Through the camera's eye we may look down Broadway in New York or inspect a prison in Chicago or pause at a corner in Hanover Junction. We can feel the heat and drabness of a textile mill or watch track layers at work or fishing boats casting their nets off Narragansett Bay. Each of these pictures represents neither an action nor a scene but a single-frame, a fleeting moment of time frozen and preserved for our imaginations to mull over.

Nothing before the camera had the power to do even that. To those who possess an insatiable appetite for knowledge of the past and of our ancestors, these frozen fragments remain a towering achievement and a precious legacy. Previously it was scarcely possible to preserve intact even the faces, structures, and artifacts of history. In that sense the advent of the camera divides the historical record into two distinct epochs: that about which we have read or heard or viewed the remains of, and that which we have glimpsed with our own eyes, if only fleetingly and in part.

It is fortunate indeed that the Civil War lies, if only barely, upon the latter side of that division. Without these photographs our sense of what life was like in those terrible years would be much the poorer.

Travel and sightseeing increased, even among the notables, and especially among the soldiers and foreign observers and dignitaries. Here Secretary of State William Seward entertains a host of diplomats in a pastoral setting. Those seated are, from the left, Molena, Nicaraguan minister; Seward; Baron de Stoeckel, Russian minister; and Mr. Sheffield, the British legation attaché. Standing from the left are Donaldson of Seward's State Department, a man unidentified, Secretary Bodesco of the Russian legation, Swedish minister Count Piper, Italian minister Bertenattie, Hanseatic minister Schleider, French minister Henri Mercier, and Lord Lyons, minister from Britain. (NA)

Main Street in Salt Lake City, Utah, October 24, 1861. Western Union, impelled largely by the war, completes the first transcontinental telegraph. Beneath the backdrop of the mighty mountains, a simple ceremony marks the occasion. With great good fortune, Western Union's "Telegraph Office" is right next to a combination liquor store and "Ambrotype Gallery." The result was this ambrotype of an historic moment. (LO)

The people of the Union played, and baseball became more and more a pastime. The New York Knickerbocker Nine in 1864. (NATIONAL BASEBALL LIBRARY)

*Russian sailors like these were a new sight in New York and San Francisco,
where the czar's fleet made showings of support for the Union.* (WRHS)

*Of course, there was no escape from the war entirely. Guns were
everywhere. A mammoth Rodman smoothbore, photographed by
Montgomery C. Meigs.* (LC)

*The mode of transporting a Rodman by rail, suspended from a bridge
truss.* (LC)

*Federal commanders did rule over certain threatened parts of the country. Major General John A. Dix exercised considerable authority over largely secessionist Maryland. (*USAMHI*)*

*Governors like Andrew Curtin of Pennsylvania initiated calls for volunteers for the Army, Curtin calling for 50,000 in 1862 and 60,000 the next year. Unlike most northern governors, he also faced the trauma of Confederate invasion of his state at Gettysburg. (*CHICAGO PUBLIC LIBRARY, SPECIAL COLLECTIONS*)*

Recruiting offices appeared in every city of any size, as here on New York's State Street. The three main buildings house the United States Quartermaster's office, but the partially obscured house on the far right has a flag in front, and a broadside offering a three-hundred-dollar bounty to men who enlist. (USAMHI)

Even on Broadway in New York the recruiters worked, and at right, behind the flag, stands the evidence of their success, an army barracks in the heart of the city. No wonder an enterprising vendor selected this spot to sell his sarsaparilla and beer at 3 cents per glass. (USAMHI)

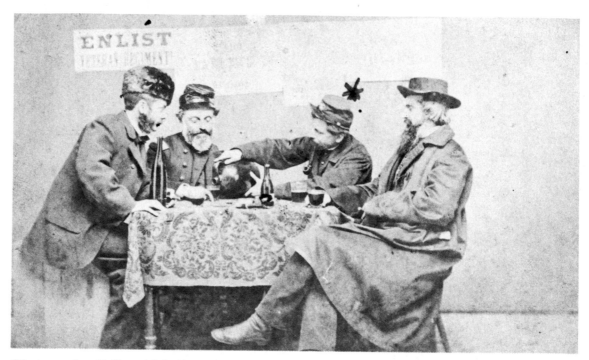

Photographer Fuller of Madison, Wisconsin, visited his local recruiter, not to enlist, but to shoot. "Enlist—Veteran Regiment" reads the broadside. Perhaps more than a few boys were induced to join after sampling the bottles and jugs, but the significance of the fencing match is, alas, lost. (USAMHI)

*All through the war the United States Military Academy at West Point
continued to produce officers for the armies.* (NA, U. S. SIGNAL CORPS)

*The cadets were eager to get to the fighting before it was ended. Many did.
Some, like Ranald Mackenzie, seated at left, would become generals. An 1862
photograph.* (USAMHI)

Two cadets of the class of 1864. They will have their chance for glory. (USAMHI)

They, like many of the generals North and South now battling all across the country, learned their military science from Professor Dennis Hart Mahan. His alumni formed a register of nearly all the high command of both armies. (USAMHI)

The Army's military posts in the North continued their functions as before, only now incredibly more busily. The second oldest post in the nation was Carlisle Barracks, Pennsylvania. Here we see guard mounting at the cavalry school of practice in 1861. Portions of the barracks behind them will be sacked by Jeb Stuart's cavalry in 1863. (T. SCOTT SANDERS)

The evidences of a nation at war were not hard to find. Fort Ellsworth in Alexandria, Virginia, named for the Union's first martyr. (USAMHI)

*Forrest Hall Military Prison in Georgetown, D.C. Next door a candy store,
with jars of peppermint sticks in the window.* (USAMHI)

Industry for the war. A Du Pont powder mill near Wilmington, Delaware.
(E. I. DU PONT DE NEMOURS & CO.)

The Schuylkill Arsenal in Philadelphia. (KA)

The blacksmith and wagon repair shop at Camp Holt, near Jeffersonville, Indiana. (INDIANA HISTORICAL SOCIETY LIBRARY)

While fighting all along its southern "borders," the Union also had to cast a careful eye to its northern boundaries, should Great Britain decide to aid the Confederacy. Then Canada would be a natural launching place for invasion. Major General John J. Peck commanded the troops along the North's Canadian frontier in 1864–65. (P-M)

In all the major cities and ports, the barracks. Fort Richmond on Staten Island,
New York. June 29, 1864. (USAMHI)

Gunboats like the U.S.S. Michigan, *the Navy's first iron-hulled warship, built in 1844, cruised the Great Lakes during the war.* (NAVAL PHOTOGRAPHIC CENTER)

But for most Northerners, the most common war experience was seeing the ever-present soldiers, either going or coming, in city and country. Hanover Junction, Pennsylvania, in November 1863, saw several, some obviously recuperating from wounds and walking with canes. (USAMHI)

In the larger cities the churches and civic groups operated entertainment centers for the soldiers home on leave or recovering from their wounds. Here the "Union Volunteer Refreshment Saloon" in Philadelphia catered to the soldiers' tastes for food and beverage, if not ladies. (I.O)

Sometimes when whole regiments came home on leave, their townsfolk entertained them royally. G. H. Houghton caught the scene in Brattleboro, Vermont, when the city welcomed home the 7th Vermont Infantry in September 1864. Arms stacked outside, the soldiers are in the Brattleboro Hotel, the building with white columns at the end of the street. While the veterans tried to forget the war for a while, the boys flocked to the street to rub their fingers over the shining bayonets of their brothers and fathers. Surely they had ventilated many a Rebel. (VERMONT HISTORICAL SOCIETY)

Happy were the men of the regiment whose enlistment expired. The 45th Massachusetts, at Readville, July 7, 1863, the day before they muster out. (MICHAEL J. HAMMERSON)

Homecoming for all too many, however, meant crepe and tears and the cold ground. It was a sight the North would become used to. (NA)

The guard of honor for the funeral of Lieutenant Colonel George E. Marshall of the 40th Massachusetts, killed at Cold Harbor, Virginia, in June 1864. Here at home in Fitchburg, even the eagle above him is draped in mourning. (USAMHI)

The Ottawa, Illinois, home of Brigadier General W. H. L. Wallace, mortally wounded at Shiloh. His portrait, his riderless horse, the flag for which he died tell the whole story. (CHS)

Finally they will come in such numbers that the government must set aside special sanctuaries for its honored dead. A. J. Russell's photograph of the military cemetery at Alexandria. (NEIKRUG PHOTOGRAPHICA, LTD.)

There, in rank upon rank, they will sleep through the ages. (NEIKRUG PHOTOGRAPHICA, LTD.)

Only on a few occasions will the North actually feel the sting of the enemy's sword, and nowhere more than in Chambersburg, Pennsylvania. In July 1864, Confederates set the torch to the town when it could not raise a ransom. The fire devastated much of the town. This view by the Zacharias brothers looks down Queen Street. (MAURICE MAROTTE, JR.)

The center of Chambersburg. Rebuilding has begun already. (MAURICE MAROTTE, JR.)

*Greater crises faced the nation than enemy raids. The men of the Supreme
Court had to deal constantly with the limits of authority in an emergency, with
habeas corpus, and the safety of the nation versus the rights of the individual.*
(NA)

*In December 1864, this military commission tried and convicted Indiana
dissenter Lambden P. Milligan of treason and sentenced him to death. The
next June, in* ex parte Milligan, *the Supreme Court would reverse that
conviction* (INDIANA STATE LIBRARY)

"Copperhead" newspapers, those seemingly disloyal or opposed to the war on whatever grounds, were often mobbed and destroyed. In Portsmouth, New Hampshire, a mob gathers in front of the States & Union office angrily denouncing its editorial stance. The sudden appearance of rain dampened their ardor, and the newspaper was not molested. (USAMHI)

Riots against the military draft in 1863 turned New York City into a bedlam, and left over 100 people dead. Lieutenant Commander Richard W. Meade, Jr., nephew of General George G. Meade, subdued the rioters. (USAMHI)

*In the North, war news came chiefly from the press, and the industry
capitalized whenever possible on the salability of the most recent news. Here on
June 9, 1862, the Pittsburgh* Dispatch *office advertises* "LATER FROM RICHMOND
& MEMPHIS, *Genl McClellan's Report of the Battle, Our loss in killed wounded
& missing 5,134." Three days before, thirteen Union and Confederate ships
met in the last fleet battle of the war at Memphis. On June 1 the Battle of Fair
Oaks in McClellan's Peninsula Campaign concluded. The* Dispatch *was
reporting both, and its billboard sign probably lists Pittsburghers injured in the
battles. The editor, Joseph Singerly Lare, appears in top hat seated at the right
on the second-floor ledge.* (MRS. ALBERT MCBRIDE)

The Dispatch *took offices above J. M. Fulton's Drug Store on Fifth Avenue.
Interested citizens gathered outside on the sidewalk for the early edition with
the latest news from the fronts.* (MRS. ALBERT MCBRIDE)

The most notorious copperhead of all was Ohio's Clement L. Vallandigham, pictured here in the center. Expelled from the Union, he went south, but Jefferson Davis did not want him either. He spent some time in Canada, then returned to Ohio in 1864, hoping vainly to cause an uprising of antiwar feeling that would defeat Lincoln at the polls. (LC)

Running against Lincoln was his one-time general, George B. McClellan. Virtually shelved after Antietam in the fall of 1862, "Little Mac" accepted the Democratic nomination in 1864. There was no beating Lincoln. (USAMHI)

*Momence, Illinois, like most other towns in the Union, saw large
demonstrations for Lincoln. He won handily.* (CHS)

*Meanwhile, the people of the North watched and waited. The ladies sewed
mammoth flags for the soldiers. These are the ladies of the Pennsylvania
Academy of Fine Arts.* (LO)

Mammoth exhibitions were held to benefit soldiers' relief organizations, like the Union Avenue fair held in Philadelphia in 1864 by the Sanitary Commission. All manner of war relics were displayed, including ship's wheels from famous vessels, cases of bullets, flags, and even photographs. (KA)

Art exhibited at the Sanitary Fair, including Emanuel Leutze's heroic depiction of Washington crossing the Delaware. (NA)

New York's great Metropolitan Fair, the largest of its kind, attracted thousands. (NA)

They saw a wondrous array of relics, displayed in that cluttered fashion so beloved of the Victorians. Here the uniform of the martyr Elmer Ellsworth, stained with his holy blood. (NA)

Captured enemy flags and relics of the battlefields. (NA)

Suppliers of military hardware displayed their stock. Here a complete exhibit of the pistols and accessories made by the Colt firearms company of Connecticut. The war made Samuel Colt a millionaire, and he sold to both sides. (NA)

Giant projectiles, swords, rifles, axes, even items totally unrelated to the war, and much of it for sale to a souvenir-hungry public. "Relics from Vicksburg Sold Here." (NA)

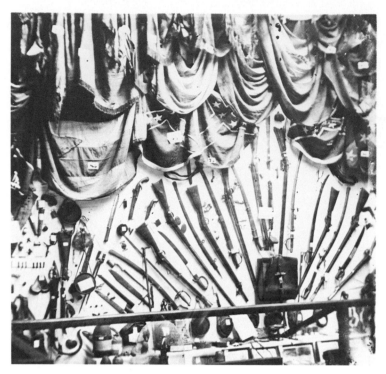

All manner of weapons, and even soldier art works, like miniature churches fashioned during the long hours in winter quarters. (NA)

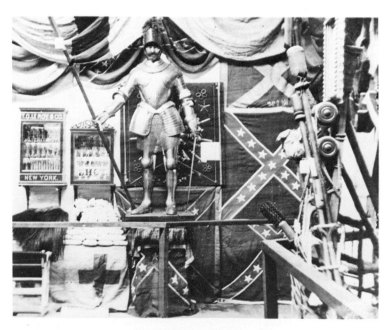

And for those not interested in the current war, a little something from an earlier era. (NA)

For those who could not see the great fairs, the photographers provided ample souvenir cartes de visite of soldiers celebrating victories. Fetter of Logansport, Indiana, captured these two sailors, one of them a double amputee, carrying a box marked "Remember Fort Fisher." For such men, pity would be their only livelihood.

(CWTI)

(DAVID FINNEY)

Another popular image, the old bugler and his dog. A Brady gallery photo taken at West Point in 1864. (LO)

Young girls shammed at soldiering for the camera, often to send to boyfriends in the Army.
(WENDELL W. LANG, JR.)

And a few women who actually passed for men or otherwise served the Army, made capital of it at home. Actress Pauline Cushman (not a very good actress) publicized widely her activities as a spy (not a very good one) in Bragg's army. (LO)

The North lived through the war and rejoiced at its end. When July 1865 came, and soldiers of Battery B, 2d United States Artillery, came to the new Soldiers National Cemetery at Gettysburg, they could look back upon the epic thus ended with some pride in their contribution to it behind the lines. (LC)

And they looked back on one who told them this time would come, and that they should look ahead "with malice toward none." Abraham Lincoln's second inauguration, March 4, 1865. Lincoln is seated, hands in his lap, just to the left of the small white lectern. On his right is Vice-President-elect Andrew Johnson. (WRHS)

The Photographers of the War

FREDERIC E. RAY

Historians with cameras and their journey for posterity

WHEN AMERICA WENT TO WAR, the camera went with it, and by 1861 neither was a stranger to the other. Photography, as an art and an industry, had already marked its first quarter century before the guns sounded. It had come a long way.

A Frenchman, Joseph-Nicéphore Niépce, experimented with the camera obscura in the 1820s and in 1826 produced probably the first successful photograph on a polished pewter plate. The exposure took eight hours. Nine years later an Englishman, Henry Fox Talbot, developed the first practical imaging process. He called it the calotype and produced it by using paper sensitized with silver salts.

But it remained for another Frenchman, one-time partner of Niépce, to make the photograph truly attainable. Louis-Jacques-Mandé Daguerre announced his "Daguerreotype" in 1839. He used a sensitized, silver-coated copper plate to capture light images in less than one half hour. Unlike Talbot, Daguerre made his methods public and the daguerreotype quickly found enthusiastic acceptance in Europe.

Thanks to two remarkable men of genius, it also found its way to America almost from the moment of creation. Samuel F. B. Morse, inventor of the telegraph, visited Daguerre in Paris in 1839 and brought back with him the process. The next year he and John W. Draper, a noted New York physicist, began experiments which led shortly to a reduction in exposure time from half an hour to half a minute. At once a lucrative portrait business mushroomed in the country, and one of the principal proponents of this new process was upstate New Yorker Mathew B. Brady, whose fashionable New York and Washington studios would soon attract the notables of the day. Before long a "Brady" became the commonplace term for a portrait.

In 1851, seven years after Brady went into business, another Englishman, Frederick Scott Archer, developed the collodion or wet-plate process. By recording his image on a glass plate, thus producing a negative, he and his revolutionary invention enabled the multiple duplication of photographs printed on salt- or albumen-treated paper, whereas the daguerreotypist could make one image, and one only. Archer's soon became the accepted process for portrait photographers, and their profession spread throughout America. By 1860 there were 3,154 photographers, ambrotypists, daguerreotypists, calotypists, melainotypists, and practitioners of other varieties of the art, spread from New York to San Francisco, from Chicago to New Orleans. The image took America by storm.

By the early 1860s almost every middle-class family owned an album, filled not only with portraits of their own, but also with copies of mass-produced images of their presidents, public figures, even actors and actresses. The carte de visite, a calling card-sized photograph ideally suited for albums—and for calling cards—became a rage. And for those wanting more realism, there was the stereoscopic view. The camera made two images simultaneously from two different lenses. They were mounted side by side on a card which, when viewed through a hand-held stereoscope, produced a three-dimensional picture. Thousands were sold to the parlors of America in the late 1850s.

With this market burgeoning just as the nation went to war in 1861, the economic potential of supplying war scenes to the public became self-evident. And others had already led the way in previous conflicts. Fifteen years before, an anonymous daguerreotypist went to Saltillo during the war with Mexico and made at least four outdoor military images that have survived. One shows Major General John E. Wool and his staff astride their horses in the streets of the city and is remarkable for its clarity. Several years later, during the Crimean War, a British artist turned photographer, Roger Fenton, employed the collodion process to capture over 350 images of the war in the Crimea.

And then the Civil War. In fact, the first artists to recognize and attempt to exploit its possibilities were southern photographers, and it is a happy thing for posterity that they did. Just a few months later the blockade so restricted the necessary imported chemicals and supplies that Confederate artists could no longer afford the highly speculative business of taking outdoor war views. After 1861 they almost exclusively used their carefully husbanded materials for the indoor portrait work that made their livelihood.

Simultaneously they descended on Charleston and Pensacola. Within days after the surrender of Fort Sumter, F. K. Houston of 307 King Street in Charleston set his camera within the parade ground of the fortress and captured it himself on his wet plates. On April 17 arrived James Osborn and F. E. Durbec of Osborn & Durbec's Southern

Stereoscopic & Photographic Depot on 223 King Street, at the "sign of the Big Camera." Their epic coverage of the fort and its environs would not be surpassed during the rest of the war. And at the same time, far away in Pensacola, Florida, J. D. Edwards of New Orleans began his own epic. Others, George S. Cook of Charleston and J. W. Petty of New Orleans, for instance, made less ambitious forays from their studios, but after the first spring of the war, they rarely did so again. Only Cook took one brief sortie in 1863, again to Sumter. For the rest of the war they would not be heard from again.

Then came Brady. "I can only describe the destiny that overruled me by saying that, like Euphorion, I felt that I had to go." So he said, and so he did. Perhaps he was urged by the example of Edwards and the others—for he and the North knew of their work—but more likely he and they had the same idea at the same time. In July 1861, excited by the prospect of capturing scenes of the then three-month-old war, he claimed to have accompanied McDowell's army on the road to Bull Run.

"I went to the first Battle of Bull Run with two wagons," he said. His innovative portable darkroom, a wagon hooded in black, was dubbed the "what-is-it" wagon. Clad in linen duster and straw hat, Brady says he "got as far as Blackburne's Ford." "We made pictures and expected to be in Richmond next day, but it was not so, and our apparatus was a good deal damaged on the way back to Washington." So Brady claimed thirty years later. In fact, no verifiable images from the first expedition have survived. Some that Brady later said were taken then, actually date months later, calling into question his entire account of his first trip to the front. Brady was first and foremost a businessman, a promoter, and his stories of many of his war exploits are highly colored by exaggeration.

Brady's eyesight was failing and he relegated the actual camera work to his assistants. He appears frequently in front of the camera in a number of his war views, but it is probable that he did not expose any images in the field himself. Throughout the war years, he only occasionally ventured to the armies, and instead spent his time in New York and Washington, supervising his flourishing portrait business and amassing the collection of views taken

*A burgeoning industry begins. In the years immediately prior to the Civil War,
the homes of Europe and America discovered the photograph. Here, in an
English shop, workers cut and mount stereoscopic views for home consumption,
and the public's appetite was voracious. The raw prints hang in the
background. The man in the white vest seated at the center is cutting them.
Ladies at the table prepare the mounting boards and glue the prints to them,
while the two boys standing at the left run the finished pieces through a press.
And even here the camera captures not just a scene, but history. Times are
starting to change. Men and women are working together in the same shop.
Yet some things have not changed, for children are working with them, too,
and the clock in the background shows it is nearly 6 P.M., with the day's work
not yet done.* (NYHS)

by his assistants and others that he would produce
as "Brady's Album Gallery" and other series. In
addition, his views were widely published by the illustrated weeklies of the day, *Harper's* and *Frank
Leslie's,* whose artists rendered the images into
woodcuts.

The men actually following the armies for Brady
were a remarkable array of artists: Alexander and
James Gardner, Timothy O'Sullivan, William Py-
well, George N. Barnard, David Woodbury, E.
Guy Foux, James F. Gibson, Stanley Morrow,
John Reekie, and several others. Some were outstanding. O'Sullivan would produce many of the
best-known war scenes. Alexander Gardner and
O'Sullivan together were unequaled in their coverage of the Army of the Potomac and both captured

resulted in loss of brilliancy and depth in the negative.

To be sure, other processes were used as well. Most of the portraits of private soldiers that were made in the camps were ambrotypes, or tintypes, cheap processes within reach of the lowly private's pocketbook. The image on a tintype was caught on a small iron sheet plated with tin and coated with black lacquer. The ambrotype was a glass negative mounted against a dark background to produce a positive image. Unlike the true print derived from the collodion negatives, daguerreotypes, ambrotypes, and tintypes, were almost always mirrored copies of the subject. This reverse image called for some simple ingenuity on the part of the photographer in posing his subjects. Accoutrements were often reversed on the person of the sitter to present them correctly in the finished picture. Even belt plates bearing the letters "US" were turned upside down, presenting a perfect "S" to be sure, but a somewhat peculiar "U."

With these hundreds of photographers traveling the country, there was little that they missed, and most of what they caught has survived. Yet, there are still the "might have been's." A Chambersburg, Pennsylvania, photographer named Bishop is supposed to have arranged his camera in a window in anticipation of the arrival of General Lee during 1863's Gettysburg Campaign. The camera at-

tracted the attention of Confederate soldiers and teamsters along the curbstones who arose to get into the image, thereby blocking Bishop's view of their general and robbing posterity of a memorable moment in time. Off Cherbourg, France, in 1864, the photographer François Rondin set up his camera and made an exposure of the battle raging at sea between the U.S.S. *Kearsarge* and the dreaded Confederate commerce raider C.S.S. *Alabama*. Seen widely at the time in the window of Rondin's Cherbourg shop, the priceless print has disappeared. A dozen or more wartime images of Abraham Lincoln are known to have been taken, but are now lost. A much rumored photograph taken from aloft in a Federal observation balloon has yet to surface, if indeed it was ever really taken.

Yet what does survive is truly staggering. An enormous debt is owed for the legacy left by those enterprising men with their little wagons, rolling over rutted roads with their fragile contents, hauling their clumsy cameras in camp and battlefield, occasionally risking their lives, and recording history as it had never been done before.

Mathew Brady, as usual, speaks for all of them, and largely it was through his energy and initiative that they all preserved for generations to come the image of the war and its people. "I felt that I had to go," he would say. "A spirit in my feet said 'Go' and I went."

Alexander Gardner's own 1863 image of his gallery on 7th and D streets, N.W., in Washington, D.C. Here one of the foremost photographers of the war made his headquarters when not in the field with the armies. Here he thumbed his nose at his one-time employer, Mathew B. Brady, whose own gallery stood nearby. While proclaiming his magnificent "Views of the War" being available on one side of his building, Gardner was a good enough businessman to devote even more advertising to the real bread and butter for all cameramen of the era, the portrait work in cartes de visite, ambrotypes, and a variety of other techniques. (LC)

Brady and Gardner had the big studios, but hundreds of others like Bowdoin, Taylor & Company's gallery at 204 King Street in Alexandria, Virginia, operated the studios that most Americans saw. Always there was the large opening in the roof to let in the sunlight essential for the camera, and always the case of samples displayed outside the front door. (T. SCOTT SANDERS)

And once the war came, the photographers proved nearly as fascinated by themselves at their work as they were with the conflict itself. Just as the Confederates fired the first shots of the war, so, too, did Confederate photographers take the first shots, both of the war and themselves. Even before the pioneering J. D. Edwards went to Pensacola, the remarkable Osborn & Durbec of King Street in Charleston captured Fort Sumter as surely and completely as did Beauregard.

Among their host of images stands this faded stereo print. It is unique, from a photographic viewpoint perhaps the most important Confederate picture from the entire war. The chief focus of attention are the men and two guns of the Trapier Mortar Battery on Morris Island, guns that bombarded Sumter. But what makes this photo so important is what lies hidden in the background. Lost for over a century and here published for the first time, this is the only known view of Confederate photographic apparatus in the field. Behind the mortar on the right stands a large pyramidal object, and just faintly visible on it are the words "Osborn & Durbec 223 King St." This is their portable darkroom, required for the speedy development of the emulsions of the era.

One of the great misfortunes of a tragic war is that the scarcity of chemicals and materials prevented artists of the caliber of Edwards and Osborn & Durbec from doing for their side of the conflict what Brady and others did for his. (TU)

Mathew B. Brady, the entrepreneurial genius who so identified himself with Civil War photography that for over a century afterward almost every Civil War image was just naturally assumed to be a "Brady." This somewhat retouched image purports to show him in field costume on July 22, 1861, the day he returned to Washington from the battlefield at Bull Run. Brady's whole story of his trip to the battle with McDowell's army is highly suspect, but the evidences of his showmanship in this photo are undeniable. Already he had begun to make Americans believe that he was the war photographer. (USAMHI)

Thanks to his failing eyesight, Brady probably spent little if any time behind the camera during the war. But he certainly spent a lot of time in front of it. In top hat he poses next to General Samuel P. Heintzelman and with members of the general's staff on the steps of Arlington House, the former home of Robert E. Lee, in Arlington, Virginia. It is the late summer of 1861, following the debacle at Bull Run. (LC)

At Blackburn's Ford, by the waters of Bull Run, two photographers pause for a glass in March 1862. (LC)

At Sudley Springs on the Manassas battlefield, the cameramen left their equipment wagon across the stream, then waded over to capture the scene, and with it their footprints in the mud. (LC)

One of the war's finest young photographers was Timothy O'Sullivan, among the first northern cameramen to return to South Carolina with the invading Federals. At Beaufort, in April 1862, he recorded an outstanding series of images, and this one probably includes himself, seated second from the right, at his "mess." (USAMHI)

Photographers went with the army of McClellan to Yorktown in May 1862.
(LC)

*Their portable darkroom intrigued a boatload of soldiers at White House on
the Pamunkey River.* (WRHS)

When the armies returned to Manassas in July 1862, so did O'Sullivan, who pauses here for a drink beside his "what's it" wagon on the Fourth of July. (LC)

Timothy O'Sullivan, "Our Artist at Manassas," the brilliant and energetic cameraman who covered most of the Civil War in the East, and later took his lenses to the West and to Central America. (LARRY J. WEST)

The equipment box in the front of the wagon says "Brady's Washington." The men are two of his numerous assistants, the one seated at left probably being David B. Woodbury, arguably the best of the artists who stayed with Brady throughout the war. (LC)

Timothy O'Sullivan's wagon stands at the end of a bridge built by McDowell's engineers across Bull Run in August 1862, just before he met defeat for the second time on the same ground. (LC)

The men who made the pictures. The first publication of a remarkable image taken at Berlin, Maryland, October 28, 1862. Standing at right is Mathew Brady. David B. Woodbury crouches to the right of him. The other assistants are, left to right, Silas Holmes, a cook named Stephen, E. T. Whitney, Hodges, and a teamster named Jim. No other surviving image from the war shows Brady and his assistants in such detail, and their equipment as well. These are some of the men who did the real work for which Brady took credit. (KA)

Linn once again at Pulpit Rock, another favorite posing place for his subjects. (KA)

Disdaining Brady's taste for notables, when Linn posed with others he selected commonplace people. Brady would never have been seen in a stovepipe hat aboard an ox-drawn wagon. (TERENCE B. O'LEARY)

Linn fascinated himself. Here he or an assistant photographs Brigadier General Thomas Sweeny, standing above the group of soldiers at left. (USAMHI)

A. D. Lytle of Baton Rouge, Louisiana, one of the most prolific of the western artists. Besides extensive portrait work, he took his camera outdoors and captured a remarkably complete record of a southern city under Union occupation. It was erroneously believed after the war that he used his camera to furnish information via photographs to the Confederates. (LSU)

Little Rock, Arkansas, in 1863 went onto emulsion for posterity in a splendid series of views taken by "White's Photograph Gallery." The studio appears at the lower right, its awninged sunlight extended toward the Arkansas River. Unusual for their striking clarity and quality, White's photographs have never been published before. (NA)

*In 1864, with the main focus of the war in the East, so was the chief focus of
the cameras. Stanley J. Morrow, a soldier stationed at the Point Lookout,
Maryland, prison camp, learned the trade—from Brady himself he would
claim—and opened his own studio. If his sunlight cover looks rather makeshift,
how much more so is his business sign. Hopefully Morrow planned his
darkroom operations better than he did the lettering for his "Picture Ga . . ."*
(STANLEY J. MORROW COLLECTION, W. H. OVER MUSEUM)

*James Gardner, brother of Alexander, one of the
many unsung true photographic artists of the war.*
(LJW)

George S. Cook, the Confederate photographer who, in 1863, braved Federal fire to take his camera out onto Fort Sumter to record the ruin caused by the enemy's bombardment. Two years before, he made the same trip to capture the images of Major Robert Anderson and his officers as they were about to become the targets of the first shots of the war. (VM)

One of Brady's photographic wagons at City Point, Virginia, during the Siege of Petersburg. A familiar sight by now, the "what's it" wagons no longer attracted the attention they once enjoyed. (NA, U. S. SIGNAL CORPS PHOTO, BRADY COLLECTION)

Three photographers lie asleep in the shade of their tent near Petersburg, their wagon in the background, while a fourth writes a letter and a Zouave private apparently wanders into the picture. (LC)

Alexander Gardner established a great reputation in the Civil War, then enhanced it by going to the Far West immediately afterward to record the opening of the new country. (LJW)

Some artists' chief official services for the War Department came in copying maps for the Topographical Engineers Corps. Here in March 1865, in front of Petersburg, a camera is ready to shoot a map for reproduction. (USAMHI)

"Photographic Wagon, Engineer Department." Perhaps part of Gardner's equipment, shown amid the bomb proofs at Petersburg in the fall of 1864. (LC)

*The goal of four years at last attained. Richmond, taken from the south side of
the James River, in April 1865. In the foreground stands a portable darkroom
and operator at work, which explains the blur of the cameraman who is
developing his image. Across the river, the large brick building, painted white
on its lower stories, is the infamous Libby Prison. An Egbert G. Foux image, an
associate of A. J. Russell.* (WRHS)

Richmond in Federal hands, and a stereo camera ready to complete the conquest. (THE MESERVE COLLECTION)

April 8, 1865, while Grant is cornering Lee at Appomattox, Brady is already in Richmond posing for his own cameras. Here at Pratt's Castle on Gambler's Hill, he stands in top hat, the war that made him great almost done. (USAMHI)

A heavily retouched photo of Messrs. Levy & Cohen of 9th and Filbert streets, Philadelphia. Their series of photographs taken in Richmond immediately after its fall are among the best produced by anyone. Levy's untimely death six months later from a heart attack prevented the firm from publishing and distributing their prints. Instead, their negatives were sold, and never presented to the public until now. (KA)

*Federal artists were quick to make use of captured Confederate photographs,
and one of their favorites was southern photographer Charles Rees's print of
Libby Prison in Richmond, taken probably in 1863. It was found after
Richmond's fall, and several northern operators published it over their own
copyright. This print was part of "Levy & Cohen's Views of the Rebel Capital
and Its Environs." It is one of the very few photographs showing Confederate
men and officers outdoors. Libby's commandant, Richard Turner, stands third
from the left in the foreground.* (KA)

*At the end of the long road, the war and the camera have come full circle.
Here at Fort Sumter they meet again in April 1865, four years after the
beginning. Samuel Cooley prepares to photograph the remnant of a once
mighty parapet. The guns are now stilled. The war's final shots belong to the
camera.* (LC)

Samuel Cooley photographs a soldier in the ruins of Fort Sumter in April 1865.
(LC)

June 10, 1865, the battlefield of the first great scene of conflict, Bull Run. Federal soldiers have come back to dedicate a monument to the memory of their brothers who fell there four years before. The photographers came with them. Sensing perhaps that this was for them, too, the end of an epoch, Alexander Gardner has had assistant W. Morris Smith capture this scene of photographers and members of the press at their liquor and cigars after the ceremonies. Gardner is seated at far left, his hand stroking his beard. S. M.

Carpenter of the New York Herald *is just to the right of him, a barrel on his knee. Standing in the center in white shirt, a dipper in his hand, is L. A. Whiteley of the* Herald. *And lying on the ground in front of him is James Gardner, brother of Alexander. Well might they celebrate, for they had seen and helped their industry come of age and, by their efforts, left a priceless record of America's most crucial moment for posterity.* (LJW)

Abbreviations

CHS	Chicago Historical Society, Chicago		NHC	Naval Historical Center
CM	Confederate Museum, New Orleans		NYHS	New-York Historical Society, New York
CWTI	Civil War Times Illustrated		OCHM	Old Court House Museum
HP	Herb Peck, Jr.		PHS	Pensacola Historical Society, Pensacola, Florida
JM	Jack McGuire			
JMB	Joe M. Bauman		P-M	Pennsylvania-MOLLUS Collection, War Library and Museum, Philadelphia
KA	Kean Archives, Philadelphia			
KHS	Kentucky Historical Society, Kentucky Military History Museum, Frankfort, Kentucky		RP	Ronn Palm
			SHC	Southern Historical Collection, University of North Carolina, Chapel Hill
LC	Library of Congress, Washington, D.C.			
LJW	Larry J. West		TU	Louisiana Historical Association, Special Collections Division, Tulane University Library, New Orleans
LO	Lloyd Ostendorf Collection			
LSU	Louisiana State University, Department of Archives and Manuscripts, Baton Rouge			
			USAMHI	U. S. Army Military History Institute, Carlisle Barracks, Pennsylvania
MC	Museum of the Confederacy		VM	Valentine Museum, Richmond, Virginia
MHS	Minnesota Historical Society		WRHS	Western Reserve Historical Society, Cleveland, Ohio
MJM	Michael J. McAfee			
NA	National Archives, Washington, D.C.			

The Contributors

The late T. HARRY WILLIAMS achieved a reputation as one of the foremost American historians of our time. His biography *Huey Long* won him the Pulitzer Prize and the National Book Award in 1969. However, he was best known for his work on the Civil War, thanks to his authorship of such books as *Lincoln and the Radicals, Lincoln and His Generals, P. G. T. Beauregard, The Union Sundered,* and many more. His chapter for *The Image of War* is one of the last productions of his prolific pen.

W. A. SWANBERG has written on a wide range of subjects in American history, from the Civil War to biographies of Jim Fisk and Theodore Dreiser. His *Citizen Hearst* was a major best-seller, and his *Luce and His Empire* won him a Pulitzer Prize for biography in 1972. His Civil War works include *Sickles the Incredible,* a biography of General Daniel Sickles, and *First Blood—The Story of Fort Sumter.*

The late BELL I. WILEY, Senior Editorial Consultant for *The Image of War,* stood preeminent among living Civil War historians, with more than fifty books that he had written or edited. The story of the common people of that era was his chief interest, and his two works *The Life of Johnny Reb* and *The Life of Billy Yank* have become classics. Dedicated in his long career to bring the past to the people of today, he served as well as chairman of the Board of Advisors of the National Historical Society.

JOSEPH P. CULLEN served for many years as a historian with the National Park Service at several of its Civil War battlefield parks. The author of innumerable articles on characters and events of that conflict, he also wrote the National Historical Society's *Concise History of the American Revolution* and *The Peninsula Campaign,* published in 1973.

VIRGIL CARRINGTON JONES has long been associated with the naval history of the war through his trilogy *The Civil War at Sea.* Yet he has covered other subjects as well, including his *Gray Ghosts and Rebel Raiders,* a history of Confederate guerrillas.

ALBERT CASTEL has specialized in the war west of the Alleghenies in three outstanding books and a host of articles. *General Sterling Price and the Civil War in the West, Kansas—A Frontier State at War,* and *William Clarke Quantrell* established his reputation as a top rank historian and writer. A major history of the Atlanta Campaign is expected soon.

LESLIE D. JENSEN, Curator of Collections at Richmond's Museum of the Confederacy, is a specialist in Confederate uniforms and equipment who has spent several years searching for the story of the elusive photographer J. D. Edwards.

MAURY KLEIN was once a student of Bell Wiley's, and continues his mentor's emphasis on sound-yet-readable history. The biographer of General E. P. Alexander, Lee's chief of artillery, Klein has also published works on the Louisville & Nashville Railroad and the Great Richmond Terminal, with a biography of Jay Gould now in progress.

FREDERIC E. RAY, a lifelong student of Civil War art and artists, is art director of *Civil War Times Illustrated* and *American History Illustrated,* as well as serving as a photographic consultant for *The Image of War.* His book *Alfred R. Waud, Civil War Artist* is probably the foremost biography yet of one of the legion of battlefield artists who followed the armies.

Index